WITHDRAWN

A BOOK OF
CHRISTMAS VERSE

Oxford University Press

London   Edinburgh   Glasgow   Copenhagen
New York Toronto Melbourne Cape Town
Bombay Calcutta Madras Shanghai
Humphrey Milford Publisher to the UNIVERSITY

A BOOK OF
CHRISTMAS VERSE

SELECTED BY
H. C. BEECHING

SECOND EDITION
REVISED

LONDON: HUMPHREY MILFORD
OXFORD UNIVERSITY PRESS
1926

Printed in England
At the OXFORD UNIVERSITY PRESS
By John Johnson
Printer to the University

PUBLISHER'S NOTE

THE original edition of *A Book of Christmas Verse* was issued in 1895. At his death in 1919 Dean Beeching left a copy of the book marked with deletions and corrections, and an amount of new matter for insertion. This revision has been carried out, and both deletions and additions have been a little increased. But substantially the book remains the same; its editor's divisions have been preserved, and the omission of his own preface to the first edition is in accord with his markings. A few poems by contemporary writers have been added.

Dean Beeching's acknowledgements for permission to use copyright poems are here reprinted from his notes:

For No. 54 to the authorities of Christ Church, Oxford; for No. 71 to Messrs. Macmillan; for No. 112 to Mr. Robert Bridges; for No. 113 to Messrs. Kegan Paul and Trench; for No. 133 to the Chiswick Press; and for No. 114 to Mr. Davidson (with an omission specially sanctioned by him). Nos. 78 and 79 (by Gerard Hopkins and Selwyn Image) appeared for the first time in this book.

For poems now appearing for the first time acknowledgements are due as follows: for No. 77, by Coventry

Patmore, to Messrs. George Bell; for No. 81, by R. L. Stevenson, to Messrs. Chatto & Windus; for No. 82, by Mrs. Meynell, to Messrs. Burns & Oates; for No. 83 to Mr. Robert Bridges; for No. 84, by Mr. Hilaire Belloc, to Messrs. Duckworth; for No. 85 (from *The Wild Knight*) to Mr. G. K. Chesterton and Messrs. Dent; for Nos. 86 and 87 to the Rev. R. L. Gales; for No. 88, by Miss Sayers, to Mr. Basil Blackwell; for No. 89 to Mr. J. D. C. Pellow; for No. 90 to Messrs. Macmillan; for No. 91 to Mrs. Chesterton; for No. 92 to Mr. Francis Keppel.

CONTENTS

Contents

viii

Contents

ix

Contents

Contents

EARLY CAROLS

WELCOME YULE

WELCOME Yule, thou merry man,
In worship of this holy day.

Welcome be thou, heaven-king,
Welcome, born in a morning,
Welcome, for whom we shall sing
Welcome Yule.

Welcome be ye, Stephen and John,
Welcome Innocents, every one;
Welcome Thomas, martyr one;
Welcome Yule.

Welcome be ye, good new year,
Welcome Twelfth day, both in fere;
Welcome Saintës, lief and dear;
Welcome Yule.

Welcome be ye, Candlemas,
Welcome be ye, Queen of bliss,
Welcome both to more or less,
Welcome Yule.

Welcome be ye that are here;
Welcome all and make good cheer;
Welcome all, another year,
Welcome Yule.

I SING of a maiden
  That is makeless; [1]
King of all kingës
  To her son she ches; [2]
He came also [3] still
  There his mother was,
As dew in April
  That falleth on the grass.
He came also still
  To his mother's bower,
As dew in April
  That falleth on the flower.
He came also still
  There his mother lay,
As dew in April
  That falleth on the spray.
Mother and maiden
  Was never none but she;
Well may such a lady
  Goddes mother be.

3.   AS JOSEPH WAS A-WALKING

AS Joseph was a-walking
  He heard an angel sing:—
'This night shall be born
  Our heavenly King;

[1] Matchless.   [2] Chose.   [3] As.

4

' He neither shall be born
  In housen nor in hall,
Nor in the place of Paradise,
  But in an ox's stall;

' He neither shall be clothed
  In purple nor in pall,
But all in fair linen
  As were babies all.

' He neither shall be rocked
  In silver nor in gold,
But in a wooden cradle
  That rocks on the mould.

' He neither shall be christened
  In white wine or red,
But with fair spring water
  With which we were christenèd.'

4.   NOW IS CHRISTËMAS YCOME

NOW is Christëmas ycome,
  Father and Son together in one,
Holy Ghost as ye be one
              In fere,
God send us a good new year.

I would you sing and I might
Of a Child is fair in sight,
His mother him bare this endris [1] night
              So still,
And as it was his will.

[1] Last.

There came three kings fro Galilee
Into Bethlem, that fair citee,
To seek him that should ever be
    By right,
Lord and king and knight.

As they came forth with their off'ring,
They met with Herod, that moody king,
    This tide,
And this to them he said,

' Of whence be ye, you kingës three?'
' Of the East, as ye may see,
To seek him that should ever be
    By right,
Lord and king and knight.'

' When you at this child have be
Come home again by me,
Tell me the sights that you have see,
    I pray,
Go you no nother way.'

They took their leave both old and ying [1]
Of Herod, that moody king:
They went forth with their offering
    By night,
By the star that shone so bright,

Till they came in to the place
Where Jesu and his mother was;
Offered they up with great solace
    In fere,
Gold and 'cense and myrrh.

     [1] Young.

When they had their offering made
As the Holy Ghost them bade,
Then were they both merry and glad
            And light :
It was a well fair sight.

Anon as they away went
The Father of heaven an angel sent
To these three Kings that made present
            This tide,
And thus to them he said,

‘ My Lord have warned you every one
By Herod king you go not home :
For an you do he will you slowe
            And strow,[1]
And do you mickle woe.’

They yeden all another way
Thorough the might of Goddes lay [2]
As the angel to them did say
            Full right :
It was a well fair sight.

When they were come to their countree
Glad and blithe they were all three
Of the sights that they had see ;
            By dene [3]
The company was clean.

Kneel we now here adown ;
Pray we in good devotiön
To the King of great renown
            For grace
In heaven to have a place.

---

[1] Lay low.   [2] Law.   [3] Forthwith.

THIS ENDRIS NIGHT

THIS endris [1] night
  I saw a sight,
A star as bright as day;
And ever among [2]
A maiden sung
    Lullay, byby, lullay.

This lovely lady sat and sang, and to her child gan say,
' My son, my brother, my father dear, why liest thou
      thus in hay?
    My sweetë brid, [3]
    Thus it is betid
      Though thou be King veray;
    But, nevertheless,
    I will not cease
      To sing byby, lullay.'

The child then spake in his talking; and to his mother
      said—
' I am beknown for heaven's king, in crib though I be laid;
    For angels bright
    Down to me light,
      Thou knowest it is no nay.
    And of that sight
    Thou mayest be light,
      To sing byby, lullay.'

[1] Last.   [2] Anon.   [3] Bird.

'Now sweetë son, since thou art king, why art thou laid
    in stall?
Why ne thou ordainèd thy bedding in some great kingës
    hall?
       Methinketh it right
       That king or knight
         Should lie in good array;
       And then among
       It were no wrong
         To sing byby, lullay.'

'Mary, mother, I am thy child, though I be laid in stall,
Lords and dukes shall worship me, and so shall kingës all.
       Ye shall well see,
       The kingës three
         Shall come the twelfthë day;
       For this behest
       Give me thy breast,
         And sing byby, lullay.'

'Now tell me, sweet son, I thee pray, thou art me lief
    and dear,
How should I keep thee to thy pay,[1] and make thee glad
    of cheer?
       For all thy will
       I would fulfil,
         Thou weet'st full well in fay.[2]
       And for all this
       I will thee kiss,
         And sing byby, lullay.'

        [1] Content.   [2] Faith.

' My dear mother, when time it be, thou take me up
      aloft,
And settë me upon thy knee, and handle me full soft.
   And in thy arm
   Thou hile [1] me warm,
    And keepë night and day;
   If I weep
   And may not sleep,
    Thou sing byby, lullay.'

' Now, sweet son, since it is so, that all is at thy will,
I pray thee grant to me a boon if it be right and skill, [2]
   That child or man
   That will or can
    Be merry upon my day;
   To bliss them bring,
   And I shall sing
    Lullay, byby, lullay.'

6. LULLAY, MY LIKING, MY DEAR SON

LULLAY, my liking, my dear son, my sweeting,
 Lullay, my dear heart, my own dear darling.

I saw a fair maiden sitten and sing.
She lulled a little child, a sweet lording.
   Lullay, &c.

That ilke lord is that that made all thing,
Of all lordës he is lord, of all kingës king.
   Lullay, &c.

    [1] Cover.   [2] Reasonable.

There was mickle melody at that childës birth,
All that were in heaven's bliss they made mickle mirth.
>   Lullay, &c.

Angels bright they sung that night and saiden to that
>   child,
Blessed be thou, and so be she that is both meek and
>   mild.
>   Lullay, &c.

Pray we now to that child, and to his mother dear.
Grant them his blessing that now maken cheer.
>   Lullay, &c.

7.   SAINT STEPHEN WAS A CLERK

SAINT STEPHEN was a clerk
In King Herodës hall,
And servèd him of bread and cloth
>   As every king befall.

Stephen out of kitchen came,
>   With boarës head on hand,
He saw a star was fair and bright
>   Over Bethlem stand.

He cast adown the boarës head
>   And went into the hall:
'I forsake thee, King Herodës,
>   And thy workës all.

Saint Stephen was a Clerk

' I forsake thee, King Herodës,
  And thy werkës all ;
There is a child in Bethlem born
  Is better than we all.'

' What aileth thee, Stephen ?
  What is thee befall ?
Lacketh thee either meat or drink
  In King Herodës hall ? '

' Lacketh me neither meat ne drink
  In King Herodës hall ;
There is a child in Bethlem born
  Is better than we all.'

' What aileth thee, Stephen ? Art thou wode [1]
  Or thou ginnest to breed ? [2]
Lacketh thee either gold or fee
  Or any richë weed ? ' [3]

' Lacketh me neither gold or fee,
  Ne none richë weed ;
There is a child in Bethlem born
  Shall help us at our need.'

' That is also [4] sooth, Stephen,
  Also sooth, i-wis, [5]
As this capon crowë shall
  That lieth here in my dish.'

---

[1] Mad.　　[2] Become (mad).　　[3] Dress.　　[4] As.　　[5] Certainly.

That word was not so soonë said,
  That word in that hall,
The capon crew, 'Christus natus est,'
  Among the lordës all.

' Riseth up, my tormentors,
  By two and also by one,
And leadeth Stephen out of this town,
  And stoneth him with stone.'

Tooken they Stephen
  And stoned him in the way,
And therefore is his even
  On Christës own day.

8.   THE SHEPHERDS' OFFERINGS

Angel. HERDMEN hend,[1]
    Dread ye no thing
Of this star that ye do see;
For this same morn
God's son is born
In Bethlem of a maiden free.

First Shepherd.

Hail maid, mother, and wife so mild!
  As the angel said, so have we fand.
I have nothing to present with thy child
  But my pipe; hold, hold, take it in thy hand;
  Wherein much pleasure that I have fand;
And now, to honour thy glorious birth,
Thou shalt it have to make thee mirth.

[1] Courteous.

The Shepherds' Offerings

Second Shepherd.

Now, hail be thou, child, and thy dame!
    For in a poor lodging here art thou laid,
So the angel said and told us thy name;
    Hold, take thou here my hat on thy head!
    And now of one thing thou art well sped,
For weather thou hast no need to complain,
For wind, ne sun, hail, snow, and rain.

Third Shepherd.

Hail be thou, Lord over water and lands!
    For thy coming all we may make mirth.
Have here my mittens to put on thy hands,
    Other Treasure have I none to present thee with.

Mary.   Now, herdmen hend,
          For your coming
          To my child shall I pray,
          As he is heaven king
          To grant you his blessing
          And to his bliss that ye may wend
             At your last day.

Here the Shepherds sing:

As I out rode this enderes [1] night
Of three jolly shepherds I saw a sight,
And all about their fold a star shone bright;
    They sang *terli, terlow*;
So merrily the shepherds their pipes can blow.

---

[1] Last.

Down from heaven, from heaven so high,
Of angels there came a great company,
With mirth and joy and great solemnity,
    They sang *terli, terlow*;
So merrily the shepherds their pipes can blow.

9.   CAN I NOT SING BUT HOY!

CAN I not sing but Hoy!
When the jolly shepherd made so much joy!

The shepherd upon a hill he sat,
He had on him his tabard and his hat,
His tar-box, his pipe, and his flagat.
His name was called Jolly, Jolly Wat;
        For he was a good herds-boy,
                Ut hoy!
        For in his pipe he made so much joy.
            Can I not sing but hoy.

The shepherd upon a hill was laid,
His dog to his girdle was tayd,
He had not slept but a little braid,
But *gloria in excelsis* was to him said;
                Ut hoy!
        For in his pipe he made so much joy!
            Can I not sing, &c.

Can I not sing but Hoy!

The shepherd on a hill he stood,
Round about him his sheep they yode,
He put his hand under his hood,
He saw a star as red as blood.
Ut hoy!
For in his pipe he made so much joy!
Can I not sing, &c.

Now farewell Mall, and also Will,
For my love go ye all still,
Unto I come again you till,
And ever more Will ring well thy bell.
Ut hoy!
For in his pipe he made so much joy!
Can I not sing, &c.

Now must I go there Christ was born,
Farewell, I come again to-morn;
Dog, keep well my sheep fro the corn,
And warn well Warroke when I blow my horn!
Ut hoy!
For in his pipe he made so much joy!
Can I not sing, &c.

When Wat to Bethlehem come was,
He sweat, he had gone faster than a pace.
He found Jesus in a simple place,
Between an ox and an ass.
Ut hoy!
For in his pipe he made so much joy!
Can I not sing, &c.

Can I not sing but Hoy!

The shepherd said anon right:
'I will go see yon ferly [1] sight,
Where as the angel singeth on-height,
And the star that shineth so bright!'
      Ut hoy!
   For in his pipe he made so much joy!
     Can I not sing, &c.

'Jesus, I offer to thee here my pipe,
My skirt, my tar-box, and my scrip,
Home to my fellows now will I skip,
And also look unto my sheep!'
      Ut hoy!
   For in his pipe he made so much joy!
     Can I not sing, &c.

'Now farewell, mine own herds-man Wat!'
'Yea, 'fore God, Lady, even so I hat! [2]
Lull well Jesus in thy lap.
And farewell, Joseph, with thy round cap!'
      Ut hoy!
   For in his pipe he made so much joy!
     Can I not sing, &c.

'Now may I well both hop and sing,
For I have been at Christ's bearing;
Home to my fellows now will I fling;
Christ of heaven to His bliss us bring!
      Ut hoy!
   For in his pipe he made so much joy!
     Can I not sing, &c.

[1] Wondrous.   [2] Am called.

C

10. WHEN CHRIST WAS BORN OF MARY FREE

WHEN Christ was born of Mary free
In Bethlem, in that fair citee,
Angels sang there with mirth and glee,
In excelsis gloria.

Herdmen beheld these angels bright,
To them appearèd with great light,
And said, ' God's son is born this night.'
In excelsis gloria.

The King is comen to save kind,
As in scripturès we find,
Therefore this song have we in mind,
In excelsis gloria.

Then, Lord, for thy great grace
Grant us in bliss to see thy face
When we may sing to thee solace,
In excelsis gloria.

11. BE WE MERRY IN THIS FEAST

BE we merry in this feast,
In quo Salvator natus est.

In Bethlehem that noble place,
As by prophecy said it was,
Of the Virgin Mary full of grace,
Salvator mundi natus est.
Be we merry, &c.

On Christmas night an angel it told
To the shepherds, keeping their fold,
That into Bethlehem with beastës wold,[1]
Salvator mundi natus est.
            Be we merry, &c.

The shepherds were compassèd right,
About them was a full great light;
'Dread ye nought', said the angel bright,
'Salvator mundi natus est.'
            Be we merry, &c.

'Behold to you we bring great joy;
For why [2] Jesus is born this day,
To us, of Mary, that mild may,[3]
Salvator mundi natus est.'
            Be we merry, &c.

And thus in faith find it ye shall,
Lying poorly in an oxes-stall.
The shepherds then God lauded all,
Quia Salvator mundi natus est.
            Be we merry, &c.

12. MAN, BE MERRY AS BIRD ON BERRY

M AN, be merry as bird on berry
And all thy care let away.

This time is born a child full good,
He that us bought upon the rood;
He bound the devil that is so wood,
            Till the dreadful doomës-day.

---

[1] Would go.   [2] Because.   [3] Maid.

When the child of mickle might
Would be born of Mary bright,
A token he sent to king and knight,
    A star that shone both night and day.

The star shone as bright as fire,
Over all the world both far and near,
In token He was without peer;
    And peerless he shall lasten ay.

The xij day come kingës three
Out of the east, with heartë free;
To worship Him they kneeled on knee
    With gold and myrrh and frankincense.

13.   ALL THIS TIME THIS SONG IS BEST

ALL this time this song is best:
Verbum caro factum est !

This night there is a child born
That sprang out of Jesse's thorn;
We must sing and say therefor
    Verbum caro factum est !

Jesus is the childës name
And Mary mild is his dame;
All our sorrow shall turn to game,
    Verbum caro factum est.

It fell upon high midnight,
The stars shone both fair and bright,
The angels sang with all their might
    Verbum caro factum est.

Now kneel we down on our knee,
And pray we to the Trinity,
Our help, our succour for to be!
    Verbum caro factum est.

14.   MATER, ORA FILIUM

MATER, ora filium
* ut post hoc exilium*
nobis donet gaudium
beatorum omnium!

Fair maiden, who is this bairn
That thou bearest in thine arm?
Sir, it is a Kingës Son,
That in heaven above doth wone.[1]
    Mater, ora, &c.

Man to father he hath none,
But Himself God alone!
Of a maiden He would be born,
To save mankind that was forlorn!
    Mater, ora, &c.

Three Kingës brought him presents,
Gold, myrrh, and frankincense,
To my Son full of might,
King of Kings and Lord of right!
    Mater, ora, &c.

[1] Dwell.

Fair maiden, pray for us
Unto thy Son, sweet Jesus,
That He will send us of His grace
In heaven on high to have a place.
Mater, ora, &c.

15. EYA, JESUS HODIE

*E*YA, *Jesus hodie*
Natus est de virgine.

Blessed be that maid Mary !
Born He was of her body ;
Goddes son that sit'th on high,
Non ex virili semine.

In a manger of an ass
Jesu lay and lulled was,
Hardë painës for to pass,
Pro peccante homine.

Kingës came from divers land
With great giftës in their hand,
In Bethlem the child they fand,
Stellae ducti lumine.

Man and child both old and young
Now in his blissful coming
To that child may we sing
Gloria tibi, Domine.

Nowel, nowel in this hall,
Make merry, I pray you all;
Unto the child may we call
   Ullo sine crimine.

16.   AVE MARIS STELLA

AVE maris stella
   The star on the sea,
Dei Mater alma
   Blessed mot [1] she be,
Atque semper virgo
   Pray thy son for me,
Felix caeli porta,
   That I may come to thee.

Gabriel that archangel,
   He was messenger;
So fair he gret our Lady
   With an 'ave' so clear:
'Hail be thou, Mary,
   Be thou, Mary,
Full of Goddes grace,
   And Queen of Mercy.'

[1] May.

*N*OËL, *Noël, Noël, Noël,*
   This is the salutation of Gabriel!

Tidings true there be come new, sent from the Trinity
By Gabriel to Nazareth, city of Galilee,
A clean maiden and pure virgin thoro' her humility
Conceived the second person in divinity.

Noël.

When he first presented was before her fair visage
In most demure and goodly wise he did to her homage
And said, 'Lady, from heaven so high, that lordës
      heritage
The which of thee born would be, I am sent on message.'

Noël.

'Hail, virgin celestial, the meekest that ever was ;
Hail, temple of deity, and mirror of all grace ;
Hail, virgin pure, I thee ensure within full little space
Thou shalt receive and Him conceive that shall bring
      great solace.'

Noël.

Then again to the angel she answered womanly,
'Whatever my lord command me do, I will obey meekly ;
Ecce sum humillima ancilla Domini,
Secundum verbum tuum, she said, *fiat mihi.*'

Noël.

OF A ROSE, A LOVELY ROSE

Of a rose, a lovely rose,
Of a rose is all my song.

Listen, lordings, both eld and ying,
How this rose began to spring;
Such a rose to my liking
  In all this world ne know I none.

The angel came from heaven's tower
To greet Mary with great honoúr,
And saidë she should bear the flower
  That should break the fiendës bond.

The flower sprung in high Bethlem,
That is bothë bright and sheen;
The rose is Mary, heaven's queen,
  Out of her bosom the blossom sprung.

The firstë branch is full of might,
That sprung on Christëmass night;
The star shone over Bethlem bright
  That is both broad and long.

The second branch sprung to hell,
The fiendës power down to fell;
Therein might none soulë dwell;
  Blessed be the time the rose sprung.

Of a Rose, a Lovely Rose

The third branch is good and swote,
It sprang to heaven crop [1] and root,
Therein to dwell and be our boot,
      Every day it showeth in priestës hand.

Pray we to her with great honoúr,
She that bare the blessed flower,
She be our help and succoúr,
      And shield us from the fiendës bond.

[1] Tip.

TRADITIONAL CAROLS

GOD rest you merry, gentlemen,
　Let nothing you dismay;
Remember Christ our Saviour
　Who was born on Christmas-day,
To save our souls from Satan's fold
　Which long time had gone astray.
　　　And 'tis tidings of comfort and joy.

From him that is our Father
　The Blessed Angel came,
And to the watchful shepherds brought
　The tidings of the same;
That there was born in Bethlehem
　The Son of God by name.
　　　And 'tis, &c.

Fear not, then said Gods Angel,
　Let nothing you affright,
This day is born a Saviour
　Of a Virgin pure and bright;
He is able to advance you
　And throw down Satan quite.
　　　And 'tis, &c.

The shepherds at these tidings
　Rejoiced much in mind,
And left their flocks a-feeding
　In tempest, storm, and wind.
And straight they went to Bethlehem
　The Son of God to find.
　　　And 'tis, &c.

29

God rest you merry, Gentlemen

But when they came to Bethlehem
    Where as our Saviour lay,
They found him in a manger,
    Where oxen fed on hay,
Our blessed Lady kneeling by
    Unto the Lord did pray.
        And 'tis, &c.

At which with sudden gladness
    The shepherds then were filled,
When as the Babe of Israel
    Thus when they had beheld.
Before his mother thus to lie
    The Scripture thus fulfilled.
        And 'tis, &c.

Now let me all of you entreat
    That are within this place,
That each dear loving Xian
    The other would embrace.
For the happy time of Xmas
    Is drawing on apace.
        With its, &c.

This version is from a broadside in the British Museum; another version is given in Sandy's *Christmas Carols* (1833), of which the last verse is:

Now to the Lord sing praises
    All you within this place;
And with true love and brotherhood
    Each other now embrace:
This holy tide of Xmas
    All others doth deface.
        With its, &c.

REMEMBER, O THOU MAN

REMEMBER, O thou man,
O thou man, O thou man,
Remember, O thou man,
  Thy time is spent.
Remember, O thou man,
How thou camest to me than,
And I did what I can :
  Therefore repent.

Remember Adam's fall,
O thou man, O thou man,
Remember, O thou man,
 From Heaven to Hell.
Remember Adam's fall,
How we were condemnèd all
To Hell perpetual
  There for to dwell.

Remember God's goodness,
O thou man, O thou man,
Remember God's goodness
  And promise made.
Remember God's goodness,
How his only Son He sent
Our sins for to redress ;
  Be not afraid !

The Angels all did sing,
O thou man, O thou man,
The Angels all did sing
  On Sion Hill ;

Remember, O thou Man

The Angels all did sing
Praise to our heavenly king
And peace to man living
   With right good will.

The shepherds amazèd was,
O thou man, O thou man,
The shepherds amazèd was,
   To hear the Angels sing.
The shepherds amazèd was,
How this should come to pass,
That Christ our Messias
   Should be our king.

To Bethlehem did they go,
O thou man, O thou man,
To Bethlehem did they go
   This thing to see;
To Bethlehem did they go
To see whether it was so,
Whether Christ was born or no
   To set us free.

As th' Angels before did say,
O thou man, O thou man,
As th' Angels before did say,
   So it came to pass.
As th' Angels before did say
They found him wrapt in hay
In a manger where he lay,
   So poor he was.

In Bethlehem was he born,
O thou man, O thou man,
In Bethlehem was he born
  For mankind dear.
In Bethlehem was he born
For us that were forlorn,
And therefore took no scorn
  Our sins to bear.

In a manger laid he was,
O thou man, O thou man,
In a manger laid he was
  At this time present.
In a manger laid he was,
Between an ox and an ass
And all for our trespass;
  Therefore repent.

Give thanks to God alway,
O thou man, O thou man,
Give thanks to God alway
  With hearts most jolly.
Give thanks to God alway
Upon this blessed day,
Let all men sing and say
  Holy, holy.

21. I SAW THREE SHIPS

I SAW three ships come sailing in
On Christmas day, on Christmas day.
I saw three ships come sailing in
 On Christmas day in the morning.

D

I saw Three Ships

And what was in those ships all three
  On Christmas day, on Christmas day?
And what was in those ships all three
  On Christmas day in the morning?

Our Saviour Christ and His lady
  On Christmas day, on Christmas day.
Our Saviour Christ and His lady
  On Christmas day in the morning.

Pray, whither sailed those ships all three
  On Christmas day, on Christmas day?
Pray, whither sailed those ships all three
  On Christmas day in the morning?

O they sailed unto Bethlehem
  On Christmas day, on Christmas day.
O they sailed unto Bethlehem
  On Christmas day in the morning.

And all the bells on earth shall ring
  On Christmas day, on Christmas day.
And all the bells on earth shall ring
  On Christmas day in the morning.

And all the angels in heaven shall sing
  On Christmas day, on Christmas day.
And all the angels in heaven shall sing
  On Christmas day in the morning.

And all the souls on earth shall sing
  On Christmas day, on Christmas day
And all the souls on earth shall sing
  On Christmas day in the morning.

Then let us all rejoice amain
  On Christmas day, on Christmas day.
Then let us all rejoice amain
  On Christmas day in the morning!

LATER POEMS
AND CAROLS

OF THE NATIVITY OF CHRIST

RORATE Coeli desuper!
Heavens, distil your balmy showers,
For now is risen the bright daystar
　From the Rose Mary, flower of flowers;
　The clear sun, whom no cloud devours,
Surmounting Phoebus in the east,
　Is comen of his heavenly towers;
Et nobis Puer natus est.

Archangels, angels, dominations,
　Thrones, potentates, and martyrs seir,[1]
And all the heavenly operations,
　Star, planet, firmament, and sphere,
　Fire, earth, air, and water clear,
To Him give loving, most and least,
　That come is in so meek maneir;
Et nobis Puer natus est.

Sinners, be glad, and penance do,
　And thank your Maker heartily,
For He, that ye might not come to,
　To you is comen full humbly,
　Your soulës with His blood to buy,
And loose you of the fiend's arrest,
　And only of His own mercy;
Pro nobis Puer natus est.

[1] Many.

Of the Nativity of Christ

Celestial fowlës in the air,
   Sing with your notes upon hight,
In firthës and forests fair.
   Be mirthful now, at all your might,
   For passed is your dully night;
Aurora has the cloudis perced,
   The sun is risen with gladsome light,
Et nobis Puer natus est.

Now spring up flowrës from the root,
   Revert you upward naturally,
In honour of the blessed fruit
   That rose up from the Rose Mary;
   Lay out your leavës lustily,
From dead take life now, at the least,
   In worship of that Prince worthy,
Qui nobis Puer natus est.

Sing heaven imperial, most of height,
   Regions of air make harmony;
All fish in floud, and fowl of flight,
   Be mirthful and make melody;
   All Gloria in Excelsis cry,
Heaven, earth, sea, man, bird, and beast,
   He that is crowned above the sky.
Pro nobis Puer natus est.

WILLIAM DUNBAR

AS I in hoary winter's night stood shivering in the snow,
Surprised I was with sudden heat which made my heart to glow;
And lifting up a fearful eye to view what fire was near,
A pretty Babe all burning bright did in the air appear.
Who scorchèd with exceeding heat such floods of tears did shed,
As though His floods should quench His flames with what His tears were fed;
Alas, quoth He, but newly born in fiery heats I fry,
Yet none approach to warm their hearts or feel my fire but I.
My faultless breast the furnace is, the fuel wounding thorns,
Love is the fire, and sighs the smoke, the ashes shame and scorns;
The fuel Justice layeth on, and Mercy blows the coals;
The metal in this furnace wrought are men's defilèd souls;
For which, as now on fire I am, to work them to their good,
So will I melt into a bath, to wash them in my blood:
With this He vanished out of sight, and swiftly shrunk away,
And straight I callèd unto mind that it was Christmas day.

ROBERT SOUTHWELL

BEHOLD a silly tender Babe,
  In freezing winter night,
In homely manger trembling lies,
  Alas! a piteous sight.

The inns are full, no man will yield
  This little Pilgrim bed;
But forced He is with silly beasts
  In crib to shroud His head.

Despise Him not for lying there,
  First what He is inquire;
An orient pearl is often found
  In depth of dirty mire.

Weigh not His crib, His wooden dish,
  Nor beast that by Him feed;
Weigh not His mother's poor attire,
  Nor Joseph's simple weed.

This stable is a prince's court,
  This crib His chair of state;
The beasts are parcel of His pomp,
  The wooden dish His plate.

The persons in that poor attire
  His royal liveries wear;
The Prince Himself is come from heaven,
  This pomp is prizèd there.

With joy approach, O Christian wight!
  Do homage to thy King;
And highly praise this humble pomp
  Which He from heaven doth bring.

                    ROBERT SOUTHWELL

25.   NEW HEAVEN, NEW WAR

COME to your heaven, you heavenly quires!
  Earth hath the heaven of your desires:
Remove your dwelling to your God,
A stall is now His best abode;
Sith men their homage do deny,
Come, angels, all their faults supply.

His chilling cold doth heat require,
Come, Seraphim, in lieu of fire;
This little ark no cover hath,
Let Cherubs' wings His body swathe;
Come, Raphael, this Babe must eat,
Provide our little Tobie meat.

Let Gabriel be now His groom,
That first took up His earthly room;
Let Michael stand in His defence,
Whom love hath linked to feeble sense;
Let Graces rock when He doth cry,
And Angels sing His lullaby.

                          41

New Heaven, New War

The same you saw in heavenly seat
Is He that now sucks Mary's teat;
Agnize [1] your King a mortal wight,
His borrowed weeds lets [2] not your sight;
Come, kiss the manger where He lies;
That is your bliss above the skies.

This little Babe so few days old
Is come to rifle Satan's fold,
All hell doth at His presence quake,
Though He Himself for cold do shake;
For in this weak unarmèd wise
The gates of hell He will surprise.

With tears He fights and wins the field,
His naked breast stands for a shield;
His battering shot are babish cries;
His arrows, looks of weeping eyes;
His martial ensigns, cold and need;
And feeble flesh His warrior's steed.

His camp is pitchèd in a stall,
His bulwark but a broken wall,
His crib His trench, hay-stalks His stakes,
Of shepherds He His muster takes;
And thus, as sure His foe to wound,
The angels' trumps alarum sound.

My soul, with Christ join thou in fight;
Stick to the tents that He hath pight;

[1] Acknowledge.   [2] Hinders.

Within His crib is surest ward,
This little Babe will be thy guard;
If thou wilt foil thy foes with joy,
Then flit not from this heavenly Boy.

ROBERT SOUTHWELL

26.   A CHILD MY CHOICE

LET folly praise that fancy loves,
    I praise and love that Child,
Whose heart no thought, whose tongue no word,
    Whose head no deed defiled.

I praise Him most, I love Him best,
    All praise and love is His;
While Him I love, in Him I live,
    And cannot live amiss.

Love's sweetest mark, laud's highest theme,
    Man's most desirèd light,
To love Him life, to leave Him death,
    To live in Him delight.

He mine by gift, I His by debt,
    Thus each to other due,
First friend He was, best friend He is,
    All times will try Him true.

Though young, yet wise; though small, yet strong;
    Though man, yet God He is;
As wise He knows, as strong He can,
    As God He loves to bless.

43

His knowledge rules, His strength defends,
　　His love doth cherish all;
His birth our joy, His life our light,
　　His death our end of thrall.

Alas! He weeps, He sighs, He pants,
　　Yet doth His angels sing;
Out of His tears, His sighs and throbs,
　　Doth bud a joyful spring.

Almighty Babe, whose tender arms
　　Can force all foes to fly,
Correct my faults, protect my life,
　　Direct me when I die!

　　　　　　　　　　　　ROBERT SOUTHWELL

27.　　　　　　　NATIVITY

IMMENSITY, cloistered in thy dear womb,
　Now leaves His well-beloved imprisonment;
There He hath made Himself to His intent,
Weak enough now into our world to come:
But oh! for thee, for Him, hath th' inn no room?
Yet lay Him in His stall, and from the orient
Stars and wise men will travel, to prevent
Th' effect of Herod's jealous general doom.
See'st thou, my soul! with thy faith's eyes, how He,
Which fills all place, yet none holds Him, doth lie!
Was not His pity towards thee wondrous high,
That would have need to be pitied by thee?
Kiss Him, and with Him into Egypt go,
With His kind mother who partakes thy woe.

44　　　　　　　　　　　　　　JOHN DONNE

FOR CHRISTMAS DAY

IMMORTAL Babe, who this dear day
Didst change Thine heaven for our clay,
And didst with flesh Thy godhead veil,
Eternal Son of God, all hail!

Shine, happy star; ye angels, sing
Glory on high to heaven's King:
Run, shepherds, leave your nightly watch,
See heaven come down to Bethlehem's cratch.

Worship, ye sages of the east,
The King of gods in meanness dressed,
O blessèd maid, smile and adore
The God thy womb and arms have bore.

Star, angels, shepherds, and wise sages,
Thou virgin glory of all ages,
Restorèd frame of heaven and earth,
Joy in your dear Redeemer's birth!

JOSEPH HALL

A HYMN ON THE NATIVITY OF MY SAVIOUR

I SING the birth was born to-night,
The Author both of life and light,
The angel so did sound it:
And like the ravished shepherds said,
Who saw the light and were afraid,
Yet searched, and true they found it.

A Hymn on the Nativity of my Saviour

The Son of God, th' Eternal King,
That did us all salvation bring,
   And freed our soul from danger;
He whom the whole world could not take,
The Word, which heaven and earth did make,
   Was now laid in a manger.

The Father's wisdom willed it so,
The Son's obedience knew no No,
   Both wills were in one stature;
And as that wisdom had decreed,
The Word was now made flesh indeed,
   And took on Him our nature.

What comfort by Him we do win,
Who made Himself the price of sin
   To make us heirs of glory!
To see this Babe, all innocence,
A martyr born in our defence:
   Can man forget the story?

BEN JONSON

30.   THE SHEPHERDS' SONG

SWEET music, sweeter far
Than any song is sweet:
Sweet music, heavenly rare,
   Mine ears, O peers, doth greet.

The Shepherds' Song

You gentle flocks, whose fleeces pearled with dew
 Resemble heaven, whom golden drops make bright,
Listen, O listen, now, O not to you
 Our pipes make sport to shorten weary night :
  But voices most divine
   Make blissful harmony :
  Voices that seem to shine,
   For what else clears the sky ?
Tunes can we hear, but not the singers see,
The tunes divine, and so the singers be.

  Lo, how the firmament
   Within an azure fold
  The flock of stars hath pent,
   That we might them behold,
Yet from their beams proceedeth not this light,
 Nor can their crystals such reflection give.
What then doth make the element so bright ?
 The heavens are come down upon earth to live :
  But hearken to the song,
   Glory to glory's King,
  And peace all men among,
   These quiristers do sing.
Angels they are, as also (shepherds) He
Whom in our fear we do admire to see.

  Let not amazement blind
   Your souls, said he, annoy :
  To you and all mankind
   My message bringeth joy.

47

The Shepherds' Song

For lo ! the world's great Shepherd now is born,
   A blessèd Babe, an Infant full of power :
After long night uprisen is the morn,
   Renowning Bethlem in the Saviour.
     Sprung is the perfect day,
       By prophets seen afar :
     Sprung is the mirthful May,
       Which winter cannot mar.
In David's city doth this Sun appear
Clouded in flesh, yet, shepherds, sit we here ?

EDMUND BOLTON

31.   OF THE EPIPHANY

FAIR eastern star, that art ordained to run
   Before the sages, to the rising sun,
Here cease thy course, and wonder that the cloud
Of this poor stable can thy Maker shroud :
Ye heavenly bodies glory to be bright,
And are esteemed as ye are rich in light,
But here on earth is taught a different way,
Since under this low roof the Highest lay.
Jerusalem erects her stately towers,
Displays her windows and adorns her bowers ;
Yet there thou must not cast a trembling spark,
Let Herod's palace still continue dark ;
Each school and synagogue thy force repels,
There Pride enthroned in misty error dwells :
The temple, where the priests maintain their quire,
Shall taste no beam of thy celestial fire,

Of the Epiphany

While this weak cottage all thy splendour takes :
A joyful gate of every chink it makes.
Here shines no golden roof, no ivory stair,
No king exalted in a stately chair,
Girt with attendants, or by heralds styled,
But straw and hay enwrap a speechless Child.
Yet Sabae's lords before this Babe unfold
Their treasures, offering incense, myrrh, and gold.

The crib becomes an altar : therefore dies
No ox nor sheep ; for in their fodder lies
The Prince of Peace, who, thankful for His bed,
Destroys those rites in which their blood was shed :
The quintessence of earth He takes, and fees,
And precious gums distilled from weeping trees ;
Rich metals and sweet odours now declare
The glorious blessings which His laws prepare,
To clear us from the base and loathsome flood
Of sense, and make us fit for angels' food,
Who lift to God for us the holy smoke
Of fervent prayers with which we Him invoke,
And try our actions in the searching fire,
By which the seraphims our lips inspire :
No muddy dross pure minerals shall infect,
We shall exhale our vapours up direct :
No storm shall cross, nor glittering lights deface
Perpetual sighs which seek a happy place.

SIR JOHN BEAUMONT

32. THE ANGELS

RUN, shepherds, run, where Bethlehem blest appears,
   We bring the best of news; be not dismayed;
A Saviour there is born more old than years,
   Amidst heaven's rolling height this earth who stayed.
   In a poor cottage inned, a virgin maid
A weakling did Him bear, who all upbears;
   There is He poorly swaddled, in manger laid,
To whom too narrow swaddlings are our spheres:
Run, shepherds, run, and solemnize His birth.
   This is that night—no, day, grown great with bliss,
   In which the power of Satan broken is:
In heaven be glory, peace unto the earth!
   Thus singing, through the air the angels swam,
   And cope of stars re-echoèd the same.

WILLIAM DRUMMOND

33. THE SHEPHERDS

O THAN the fairest day, thrice fairer night!
   Night to blest days in which a sun doth rise,
   Of which that golden eye which clears the skies
Is but a sparkling ray, a shadow-light!
And blessèd ye, in silly pastor's sight,
   Mild creatures, in whose warm crib now lies
That heaven-sent Youngling, holy-maid-born Wight,
Midst, end, beginning of our prophecies!

50

The Shepherds

Blest cottage that hath flowers in winter spread,
  Though withered—blessèd grass that hath the grace
  To deck and be a carpet to that place!
Thus sang, unto the sounds of oaten reed,
  Before the Babe, the shepherds bowed on knees,
  And springs ran nectar, honey dropped from trees.

WILLIAM DRUMMOND

34.   A ROCKING HYMN

SWEET baby, sleep! What ails my dear?
    What ails my darling thus to cry?
Be still, my child, and lend thine ear
    To hear me sing thy lullaby.
        My pretty lamb, forbear to weep;
        Be still, my dear; sweet baby, sleep!

Thou blessèd soul, what canst thou fear?
    What thing to thee can mischief do?
Thy God is now thy Father dear;
    His holy spouse thy mother too.
        Sweet baby, then, forbear to weep;
        Be still, my babe; sweet baby, sleep!

Whilst thus thy lullaby I sing,
    For thee great blessings ripening be;
Thine Eldest Brother is a King,
    And hath a kingdom bought for thee.
        Sweet baby, then, forbear to weep;
        Be still, my babe; sweet baby, sleep.

A Rocking Hymn

Sweet baby, sleep, and nothing fear;
   For whosoever thee offends
By thy protector threatened are,
   And God and angels are thy friends.
      Sweet baby, then, forbear to weep;
      Be still, my babe; sweet baby, sleep.

When God with us was dwelling here,
   In little babes He took delight:
Such innocents as thou, my dear,
   Are ever precious in His sight.
      Sweet baby, then, forbear to weep;
      Be still, my babe; sweet baby, sleep.

A little Infant once was He,
   And strength in weakness then was laid
Upon His virgin-mother's knee,
   That power to thee might be conveyed.
      Sweet baby, then, forbear to weep;
      Be still, my babe; sweet baby, sleep.

In this thy frailty and thy need
   He friends and helpers doth prepare,
Which thee shall cherish, clothe, and feed,
   For of thy weal they tender are.
      Sweet baby, then, forbear to weep;
      Be still, my babe; sweet baby, sleep.

The King of kings, when He was born,
   Had not so much for outward ease;
By Him such dressings were not worn,
   Nor such-like swaddling-clothes as these.
      Sweet baby, then, forbear to weep;
      Be still, my babe; sweet baby, sleep.

Within a manger lodged thy Lord,
    Where oxen lay and asses fed ;
Warm rooms we do to thee afford,
    An easy cradle or a bed.
        Sweet baby, then, forbear to weep ;
        Be still, my babe ; sweet baby, sleep.

The wants that He did then sustain
    Have purchased wealth, my babe, for thee ;
And by His torments and His pain
    Thy rest and ease securèd be.
        My baby, then, forbear to weep ;
        Be still, my babe ; sweet baby, sleep.

Thou hast, yet more, to perfect this,
    A promise and an earnest got
Of gaining everlasting bliss,
    Though thou, my babe, perceiv'st it not.
        Sweet baby, then, forbear to weep ;
        Be still, my babe ; sweet baby, sleep.

                        GEORGE WITHER

35.   GLORIA IN EXCELSIS

AS on the night before this happy morn,
  A blessèd angel unto shepherds told
Where (in a stable) He was poorly born,
Whom nor the earth nor heaven of heavens can hold :
    Thro' Bethlehem rung
      This news at their return ;
    Yea, angels sung
      That God with us was born ;
And they made mirth because we should not mourn.

Their angel carol sing we, then,
> To God on high all glory be,
> For peace on earth bestoweth He,
And sheweth favour unto men.

This favour Christ vouchsafèd for our sake;
> To buy us thrones, He in a manger lay;
Our weakness took, that we His strength might take;
> And was disrobed that He might us array;
> > Our flesh He wore,
> > > Our sin to wear away;
> > Our curse He bore,
> > > That we escape it may;
And wept for us, that we might sing for aye.
> > With angels therefore, sing again,
> > To God on high all glory be,
> > For peace on earth bestoweth He,
And sheweth favour unto men.

GILES FLETCHER

36.   WHO CAN FORGET?

WHO can forget—never to be forgot—
> The time, that all the world in slumber lies,
When, like the stars, the singing angels shot
To earth, and heaven awakèd all his eyes
To see another sun at midnight rise
> On earth? Was never sight of pareil fame,
> For God before man like Himself did frame,
But God Himself now like a mortal man became.

Who can Forget?

A Child He was, and had not learnt to speak,
That with His word the world before did make;
His mother's arms Him bore, He was so weak,
That with one hand the vaults of heaven could shake,
See how small room my infant Lord doth take,
　　Whom all the world is not enough to hold!
　　Who of His years, or of His age hath told?
Never such age so young, never a child so old.

And yet but newly He was infanted,
And yet already He was sought to die;
Yet scarcely born, already banishèd;
Not able yet to go, and forced to fly:
But scarcely fled away, when by and by
　　The tyrant's sword with blood is all defiled,
　　And Rachel, for her sons, with fury wild,
Cries, 'O thou cruel king, and O my sweetest child!'

Egypt His nurse became, where Nilus springs,
Who, straight to entertain the rising sun,
The hasty harvest in his bosom brings;
But now for drought the fields were all undone,
And now with waters all is overrun:
　　So fast the Cynthian mountains poured their snow,
　　When once they felt the sun so near them glow,
That Nilus Egypt lost, and to a sea did grow.

The angels carolled loud their song of peace;
The cursèd oracles were strucken dumb;
To see their Shepherd the poor shepherds press;
To see their King the kingly sophies come;
And them to guide unto his Master's home,

Who can Forget?

A star comes dancing up the orient,
That springs for joy over the strawy tent,
Where gold, to make their Prince a crown, they all
    present.

GILES FLETCHER

37.   A CHRISTMAS CAROL

[Sung to the King in the Presence at Whitehall.]

Chorus.

WHAT sweeter music can we bring
    Than a carol, for to sing
The birth of this our heavenly King?
Awake the voice! awake the string!
Heart, ear, and eye, and every thing
Awake! the while the active finger
Runs division with the singer.

[From the flourish they come to the song.]

1. Dark and dull night, fly hence away,
    And give the honour to this day,
    That sees December turn'd to May.

2. If we may ask the reason, say
    The why and wherefore all things here
    Seem like the spring-time of the year?

3. Why does the chilling winter's morn
    Smile like a field beset with corn?
    Or smell like to a mead new shorn,
      Thus on the sudden?   4. Come and see
      The cause why things thus fragrant be:

'Tis He is born whose quickening birth
Gives life and lustre, public mirth,
To heaven and the under-earth.

> *Chorus.*
> We see Him come, and know Him ours,
> Who with His sunshine and His showers
> Turns all the patient ground to flowers.

1. The Darling of the world is come,
   And fit it is we find a room
   To welcome Him.   2. The nobler part
   Of all the house here is the heart.

> *Chorus.*
> Which we will give Him; and bequeath
> This holly and this ivy wreath,
> To do Him honour; who's our King,
> And Lord of all this revelling.

ROBERT HERRICK

38.   AN ODE ON THE BIRTH OF OUR SAVIOUR

IN numbers, and but these few,
I sing Thy birth, O Jesu!
Thou pretty Baby, born here
With sup'rabundant scorn here:
Who for Thy princely port here,
        Hadst for Thy place
        Of birth, a base
Out-stable for Thy court here.

An Ode on the Birth of our Saviour

Instead of neat enclosures
Of interwoven osiers,
Instead of fragrant posies
Of daffodils and roses,
Thy cradle, kingly Stranger,
  As gospel tells,
  Was nothing else
But here a homely manger.

But we with silks, not crewels,
With sundry precious jewels,
And lily work will dress Thee;
And, as we dispossess Thee
Of clouts, we'll make a chamber,
  Sweet Babe, for Thee,
  Of ivory,
And plastered round with amber.

The Jews they did disdain Thee,
But we will entertain Thee,
With glories to await here
Upon Thy princely state here,
And more for love than pity.
  From year to year
  We'll make Thee here
A free-born of our city.

ROBERT HERRICK

ALL after pleasures as I rid one day,
My horse and I both tired, body and mind,
With full cry of affections quite astray,
I took up in the next inn I could find.

There, when I came, whom found I but my dear—
My dearest Lord; expecting till the grief
Of pleasures brought me to Him; ready there
To be all passengers' most sweet relief?

O Thou, whose glorious, yet contracted, light,
Wrapt in night's mantle, stole into a manger;
Since my dark soul and brutish is Thy right,
To man, of all beasts, be not Thou a stranger.

Furnish and deck my soul, that Thou may'st have
A better lodging than a rack or grave.

The shepherds sing; and shall I silent be?
My God, no hymn for thee?
My soul's a shepherd too; a flock it feeds
Of thoughts and words and deeds.
The pasture is Thy word, the streams Thy grace,
Enriching every place.

Shepherd and flock shall sing, and all my powers
Outsing the daylight hours.
Then we will chide the sun for letting night
Take up his place and right:
We sing one common Lord; wherefore he should
Himself the candle hold.

I will go searching till I find a sun
   Shall stay till we have done;
A willing shiner, that shall shine as gladly
   As frost-nipt suns look sadly.
Then we will sing and shine all our own day,
   And one another pay.

His beams shall cheer my breast, and both so twine,
Till ev'n His beams sing and my music shine.

GEORGE HERBERT

40. ON THE MORNING OF CHRIST'S NATIVITY

THIS is the month, and this the happy morn,
   Wherein the Son of heaven's eternal King,
Of wedded Maid and Virgin-Mother born,
Our great redemption from above did bring;
For so the holy sages once did sing,
     That He our deadly forfeit should release,
And with His Father work us a perpetual peace.

That glorious form, that light unsufferable,
And that far-beaming blaze of majesty,
Wherewith He wont at heaven's high council-table
To sit the midst of Trinal Unity,
He laid aside; and, here with us to be,
     Forsook the courts of everlasting day,
And chose with us a darksome house of mortal clay.

Say, heavenly Muse, shall not thy sacred vein
Afford a present to the Infant God?
Hast thou no verse, no hymn, or solemn strain,

To welcome Him to this His new abode,
Now while the heaven, by the sun's team untrod,
    Hath took no print of the approaching light,
And all the spangled host keep watch in squadrons
      bright?

See, how from far, upon the eastern road,
The star-led wizards haste with odours sweet;
O run, prevent them with thy humble ode,
And lay it lowly at His blessed feet;
Have thou the honour first thy Lord to greet,
    And join thy voice unto the angel-quire,
From out His secret altar touch'd with hallow'd fire.

THE HYMN

It was the winter wild,
While the heaven-born Child
    All meanly wrapt in the rude manger lies;
Nature in awe to Him,
Had doff'd her gaudy trim,
    With her great Master so to sympathize:
It was no season then for her
To wanton with the sun, her lusty paramour.

Only with speeches fair,
She woos the gentle air
    To hide her guilty front with innocent snow,
And on her naked shame,
Pollute with sinful blame,
    The saintly veil of maiden-white to throw;
Confounded, that her Maker's eyes
Should look so near upon her foul deformities.

But He, her fears to cease,
Sent down the meek-eyed Peace;
    She, crown'd with olive green, came softly sliding
Down through the turning sphere,
His ready harbinger,
    With turtle wing the amorous clouds dividing;
And waving wide her myrtle wand,
She strikes a universal peace through sea and land.

No war, or battle's sound,
Was heard the world around:
    The idle spear and shield were high up-hung,
The hooked chariot stood
Unstain'd with hostile blood;
    The trumpet spake not to the armed throng,
And kings sat still with awful eye,
As if they surely knew their sovran Lord was by.

But peaceful was the night
Wherein the Prince of Light
    His reign of peace upon the earth began:
The winds with wonder whist
Smoothly the waters kist,
    Whispering new joys to the mild ocean,
Who now hath quite forgot to rave,
While birds of calm sit brooding on the charmed wave.

The stars with deep amaze
Stand fix'd in steadfast gaze,

On the Morning of Christ's Nativity

    Bending one way their precious influence,
And will not take their flight
For all the morning light,
    Or Lucifer that often warn'd them thence;
But in their glimmering orbs did glow,
Until their Lord Himself bespake, and bid them go.

    And though the shady gloom
Had given day her room,
    The sun himself withheld his wonted speed,
And hid his head for shame,
As his inferior flame
    The new enlighten'd world no more should need;
He saw a greater Sun appear
Than his bright throne, or burning axletree could bear.

    The shepherds on the lawn,
Or ere the point of dawn,
    Sat simply chatting in a rustic row;
Full little thought they then
That the mighty Pan
    Was kindly come to live with them below;
Perhaps their loves, or else their sheep,
Was all that did their silly thoughts so busy keep.

    When such music sweet
Their hearts and ears did greet,
    As never was by mortal finger strook;
Divinely-warbled voice
Answering the stringed noise,
    As all their souls in blissful rapture took:

The air such pleasure loth to lose,
With thousand echoes still prolongs each heavenly close.

Nature that heard such sound,
Beneath the hollow round
    Of Cynthia's seat, the airy region thrilling,
Now was almost won
To think her part was done,
    And that her reign had here its last fulfilling;
She knew such harmony alone
Could hold all heaven and earth in happier union.

At last surrounds their sight
A globe of circular light,
    That with long beams the shamefac'd night array'd,
The helmed Cherubim,
And sworded Seraphim,
    Are seen in glittering ranks with wings display'd,
Harping in loud and solemn quire,
With unexpressive notes to Heaven's new-born Heir.

Such music (as 'tis said)
Before was never made,
    But when of old the sons of morning sung,
While the Creator great
His constellations set,
    And the well-balanced world on hinges hung,
And cast the dark foundations deep,
And bid the weltering waves their oozy channel keep.

On the Morning of Christ's Nativity

Ring out, ye crystal spheres,
Once bless our human ears,
    (If ye have power to touch our senses so;)
And let your silver chime
Move in melodious time,
     And let the base of heaven's deep organ blow;
And with your ninefold harmony
Make up full consort to th' angelic symphony.

For if such holy song
Enwrap our fancy long,
    Time will run back, and fetch the age of gold;
And speckled Vanity
Will sicken soon and die,
    And leprous Sin will melt from earthly mould;
And Hell itself will pass away,
And leave her dolorous mansions to the peering day.

Yea, Truth and Justice then
Will down return to men,
    Orb'd in a rainbow; and, like glories wearing,
Mercy will sit between,
Thron'd in celestial sheen,
    With radiant feet the tissued clouds down steering;
And heaven, as at some festival,
Will open wide the gates of her high palace-hall.

But wisest Fate says no,
This must not yet be so,

The Babe lies yet in smiling infancy,
That on the bitter cross
Must redeem our loss;
    So both Himself and us to glorify:
Yet first to those ychain'd in sleep,
The wakeful trump of doom must thunder through the
      deep,

With such a horrid clang
As on Mount Sinai rang.
    While the red fire and smouldering clouds outbrake:
The aged earth aghast
With terror of that blast,
    Shall from the surface to the centre shake;
When at the world's last session,
The dreadful Judge in middle air shall spread his throne.

And then at last our bliss
Full and perfect is,
    But now begins; for from this happy day
The old dragon under ground
In straiter limits bound,
    Not half so far casts his usurped sway,
And wroth to see his kingdom fail,
Swinges the scaly horror of his folded tail.

The oracles are dumb,
No voice or hideous hum
    Runs through the arched roof in words deceiving
Apollo from his shrine
Can no more divine,
    With hollow shriek the steep of Delphos leaving.

No nightly trance, or breathed spell,
Inspires the pale-eyed priest from the prophetic cell.

The lonely mountains o'er,
And the resounding shore,
    A voice of weeping heard, and loud lament;
From haunted spring and dale,
Edg'd with poplar pale,
    The parting Genius is with sighing sent;
With flower-inwoven tresses torn,
The Nymphs in twilight shade of tangled thickets mourn.

In consecrated earth
And on the holy hearth
    The Lars and Lemures moan with midnight plaint;
In urns and altars round,
A drear and dying sound
    Affrights the Flamens at their service quaint;
And the chill marble seems to sweat,
While each peculiar power forgoes his wonted seat.

Peor and Baälim
Forsake their temples dim,
    With that twice batter'd god of Palestine;
And mooned Ashtaroth,
Heaven's queen and mother both,
    Now sits not girt with tapers' holy shine;
The Libyc Hammon shrinks his horn,
In vain the Tyrian maids their wounded Thammuz
      mourn.

And sullen Moloch, fled,
Hath left in shadows dread
    His burning idol all of blackest hue ;
In vain with cymbals' ring
They call the grisly king,
    In dismal dance about the furnace blue ;
The brutish gods of Nile as fast,
Isis, and Orus, and the dog Anubis, haste.

Nor is Osiris seen
In Memphian grove or green,
    Trampling the unshower'd grass with lowings loud :
Nor can he be at rest
Within his sacred chest,
    Naught but profoundest hell can be his shroud ;
In vain with timbrell'd anthems dark
The sable-stoled sorcerers bear his worshipt ark.

He feels from Juda's land
The dreaded Infant's hand ;
    The rays of Bethlehem blind his dusky eyn ;
Nor all the gods beside
Longer dare abide,
    Not Typhon huge ending in snaky twine :
Our Babe, to show His Godhead true,
Can in His swaddling bands control the damned crew.

So when the sun in bed,
Curtain'd with cloudy red,

Pillows his chin upon an orient wave,
The flocking shadows pale
Troop to th' infernal jail;
    Each fetter'd ghost slips to his several grave,
And the yellow-skirted Fays
Fly after the night-steeds, leaving their moon-loved maze.

But see the Virgin blest
Hath laid her Babe to rest;
    Time is our tedious song should here have ending,
Heaven's youngest-teemed star
Hath fix'd her polish'd car,
    Her sleeping Lord with handmaid lamp attending:
And all about the courtly stable
Bright-harness'd angels sit in order serviceable.

JOHN MILTON

41.   A HYMN OF THE NATIVITY

Chorus.

COME we shepherds whose blest sight
   Hath met Love's noon in Nature's night,
Come, lift we up our loftier song,
And wake the sun that lies too long.

To all our world of well-stol'n joy,
   He slept and dreamt of no such thing,
While we found out heaven's fairer eye
   And kist the cradle of our King;
Tell him he rises now too late,
To show us aught worth looking at.

A Hymn of the Nativity

Tell him we now can show him more
  Than e'er he showed to mortal sight,
Than he himself e'er saw before,
  Which to be seen needs not his light.
Tell him, Tityrus, where th' hast been,
Tell him, Thyrsis, what th' hast seen.

Tityrus.

Gloomy night embraced the place
  Where the noble Infant lay,
The Babe looked up and showed His face;
  In spite of darkness it was day.
It was Thy day, Sweet, and did rise
Not from the East but from Thine eyes.
  Chorus.—It was Thy day, Sweet, &c.

Thyrsis.

Winter chid aloud and sent
  The angry North to wage his wars,
The North forgot his fierce intent,
  And left perfumes instead of scars;
By those sweet eyes' persuasive powers,
Where he meant frost he scattered flowers.
  Chorus.—By those sweet eyes, &c.

Both.

We saw Thee in Thy balmy nest,
  Bright dawn of our eternal day!
We saw Thine eyes break from their East
  And chase the trembling shades away:
We saw Thee and we blest the sight,
We saw Thee by Thine own sweet light.

A Hymn of the Nativity

Tityrus.

Poor world (said I), what wilt thou do
  To entertain this starry Stranger?
Is this the best thou canst bestow,
  A cold and not too cleanly manger?
Contend, ye powers of heaven and earth,
To fit a bed for this huge birth.
    Chorus.—Contend, ye powers, &c.

Thyrsis.

Proud world (said I), cease your contest,
  And let the mighty Babe alone,
The Phoenix builds the Phoenix' nest,
  Love's architecture is all one.
The Babe whose birth embraves this morn,
Made His own bed ere He was born.
    Chorus.—The Babe whose birth, &c.

Tityrus.

I saw the curl'd drops, soft and slow,
  Come hovering o'er the place's head,
Offering their whitest sheets of snow
  To furnish the fair Infant's bed:
Forbear (said I), be not too bold;
Your fleece is white, but 'tis too cold.
    Chorus.—Forbear (said I), &c.

Thyrsis.

I saw the obsequious seraphins
  Their rosy fleece of fire bestow;

For well they now can spare their wings,
  Since heaven itself lies here below :
Well done (said I), but are you sure
Your down so warm will pass for pure ?
    Chorus.—Well done (said I), &c.

Tityrus.

No, no, your King's not yet to seek
  Where to repose His royal head.
See, see, how soon His new-bloom'd cheek
  Twixt's mother's breasts is gone to bed :
Sweet choice (said I), no way but so,
Not to lie cold, yet sleep in snow.
    Chorus.—Sweet choice (said I), &c.

Both.

We saw Thee in Thy balmy nest,
  Bright dawn of our eternal day !
We saw Thine eyes break from their East
  And chase the trembling shades away ;
We saw Thee and we blest the sight,
We saw Thee by Thine own sweet light.
    Chorus.—We saw Thee, &c.

Full Chorus.

Welcome all wonder in one sight,
  Eternity shut in a span,
Summer in winter, day in night,
  Heaven in earth and God in man !
Great little One ! whose all-embracing birth
Lifts earth to heaven, stoops heaven to earth.

A Hymn of the Nativity

Welcome, though not to gold nor silk
    To more than Caesar's birthright is,
Two sister seas of virgin milk,
    With many a rarely-tempered kiss,
That breathes at once both maid and mother,
Warms in the one and cools in the other.

She sings thy tears asleep, and dips
    Her kisses in thy weeping eye;
She spreads the red leaves of thy lips
    That in their buds yet blushing lie:
She 'gainst those mother-diamonds tries
The points of her young eagle's eyes.

Welcome, though not to those gay flies
    Gilded i' the beams of earthly kings,
Slippery souls in smiling eyes,
    But to poor shepherds' home-spun things;
Whose wealth's their flock, whose wit to be
Well read in their simplicity.

Yet when young April's husband-showers
    Shall bless the fruitful Maia's bed,
We'll bring the first-born of her flowers
    To kiss Thy feet and crown Thy head:
To Thee, dread Lamb, whose love must keep
The shepherds more than they their sheep.

To Thee, meek Majesty! soft King
    Of simple graces and sweet loves,

Each of us his lamb will bring,
　　Each his pair of silver doves,
Till burnt at last in fire of Thy fair eyes,
　Ourselves become our own best sacrifice.

RICHARD CRASHAW

42.　SATAN'S SIGHT OF THE NATIVITY

HEAVEN'S golden-wingèd herald late he saw
　To a poor Galilean virgin sent:
How long the bright youth bowed, and with what
　　　awe
Immortal flowers to her fair hand present.
He saw th' old Hebrew's womb neglect the law
Of age and barrenness, and her babe prevent
　　His birth by his devotion, who began
　　Betimes to be a saint, before a man.

He saw rich nectar thaws release the rigour
Of th' icy north, from frost-bound Atlas' hands
His adamantine fetters fall; green vigour
Gladding the Scythian rocks and Libyan sands.
He saw a vernal smile sweetly disfigure
Winter's sad face, and through the flowery lands
　　Of fair Engaddi's honey-sweating fountains
　　With manna, milk, and balm new broach the
　　　mountains.

Satan's Sight of the Nativity

He saw how in that blest day-bearing night
The heaven rebukèd shades made haste away;
How bright a dawn of angels with new light
Amazed the midnight world, and made a day
Of which the morning knew not; mad with spight
He mark'd how the poor shepherds ran to pay
    Their simple tribute to the Babe, whose birth
    Was the great business both of heaven and earth.

He saw a threefold sun with rich increase
Make proud the ruby portals of the East,
He saw the temple sacred to sweet peace
Adore her Prince's birth flat on her breast.
He saw the falling idols all confess
A coming Deity.   He saw the nest
    Of poisonous and unnatural loves, earth-nurst,
    Touch'd with the world's true antidote, to burst.

He saw heaven blossom with a new-born light,
On which, as on a glorious stranger, gazed
The golden eyes of night, whose beam made bright
The way to Bethlem; and as boldly blazed
(Nor ask'd leave of the sun) by day as night.
By whom (as heaven's illustrious handmaid) raised
Three kings or, what is more, three wise men went
Westward to find the world's true orient.

.   .   .   .

Satan's Sight of the Nativity

That the great angel-blinding light should shrink
His blaze to shine in a poor shepherd's eye,
That the unmeasured God so low should sink
As Pris'ner in a few poor rags to lie,
That from His mother's breast He milk should drink
Who feeds with nectar heaven's fair family,
    That a vile manger His low bed should prove
    Who in a throne of stars thunders above:

That He, whom the sun serves, should faintly peep
Through clouds of infant flesh; that He the old
Eternal Word should be a Child and weep,
That He who made the fire should fear the cold:
That heaven's high majesty His court should keep
In a clay cottage, by each blast controll'd:
    That glory's self should serve our griefs and fears,
    And free Eternity submit to years;

And further, that the law's eternal Giver
Should bleed in His own law's obedience;
And to the circumcising knife deliver
Himself, the forfeit of His slave's offence;
That the unblemish'd Lamb, blessed for ever,
Should take the mark of sin, and pain of sense:—
    These are the knotty riddles, whose dark doubt
    Entangle his lost thoughts past getting out.

RICHARD CRASHAW (from *Sospetto d'Herode*)

43. A HYMN FOR THE EPIPHANY

[Sung as by the three kings.]

1st King.

BRIGHT Babe! whose awful beauties make
The morn incur a sweet mistake;

2nd King.

For whom the officious heavens devise
To disinherit the sun's rise;

3rd King.

Delicately to displace
The day, and plant it fairer in thy face;

1st King.

O Thou born King of loves!

2nd King.   Of lights!

3rd King.   Of joys!

Chorus.

Look up, sweet Babe, look up and see!
For love of Thee,
Thus far from home,
The East is come
To seek herself in Thy sweet eyes.

1st King.

We who strangely went astray,
Lost in a bright
Meridian night;

2nd King.

A darkness made of too much day;

3rd King.

Beckoned from far,

By thy fair star,

Lo, at last have found our way.

Chorus.

To thee, thou Day of Night; thou East of West!

Lo, we at last have found the way

To thee, the world's great universal East,

The general and indifferent day.

1st King.

All-circling point! all-centring sphere!

The world's one, round, eternal year:

2nd King.

Whose full and all-unwrinkled face,

Nor sinks nor swells, with time or place;

3rd King.

But everywhere and every while

Is one consistent solid smile.

1st King.

Not vexed and tost,

2nd King.

'Twixt spring and frost;

3rd King.

Nor by alternate shreds of light,

Sordidly shifting hands with shades and night.

Chorus.

O little All, in Thy embrace,

The world lies warm and likes his place;

Nor does his full globe fail to be

Kissed on both his cheeks by Thee;

A Hymn for the Epiphany

Time is too narrow for Thy year,
Nor makes the whole world Thy half-sphere.

. . . .

Therefore, to Thee, and Thine auspicious ray,
(Dread sweet !), lo thus,
At least by us,
The delegated eye of day,
Does first his sceptre, then himself, in solemn tribute pay:
Thus he undresses
His sacred unshorn tresses;
At thy adorèd feet thus he lays down,
1st King.
His glorious tire
Of flame and fire,
2nd King.   His glittering robe,
3rd King.   His sparkling crown,
1st King.   His gold,
2nd King.   His myrrh,
3rd King.   His frankincense.
Chorus.
To which he now has no pretence;
For being show'd by this day's light, how far
He is from sun, enough to make thy star,
His best ambition now is but to be
Something a brighter shadow, sweet ! of thee.
Or on heaven's azure forehead high to stand,
Thy golden index; with a duteous hand
Pointing us home to our own Sun,
The world's and his Hyperion.

RICHARD CRASHAW

44. HYMN FOR CHRISTMAS DAY

[Being a dialogue between three shepherds.]

1st.

WHERE is this blessed Babe
 That hath made
All the world so full of joy
 And expectation;
 That glorious Boy
 That crowns each nation
With a triumphant wreath of blessedness?

2nd.

Where should He be but in the throng,
 And among
His angel ministers, that sing
 And take wing
Just as may echo to His voice,
 And rejoice,
When wing and tongue and all
May so procure their happiness?

3rd.

But He hath other waiters now:
 A poor cow,
An ox and mule, stand and behold,
 And wonder
That a stable should enfold
 Him that can thunder.
 Chorus.—O what a gracious God have we,
How good! how great! even as our misery.

JEREMY TAYLOR

AWAKE, my soul, and come away:
  Put on thy best array;
   Lest if thou longer stay
Thou lose some minutes of so blest a day.
         Go run,
And bid good-morrow to the sun;
Welcome his safe return
         To Capricorn,
   And that great morn
   Wherein a God was born,
   Whose story none can tell
But He whose every word's a miracle.

To-day Almightiness grew weak;
The Word itself was mute and could not speak.

That Jacob's star which made the sun
To dazzle if he durst look on,
Now mantled o'er in Bethlehem's night,
Borrowed a star to show him light.
He that begirt each zone,
To whom both poles are one,
Who grasped the zodiac in his hand
And made it move or stand,
Is now by nature man,
By stature but a span;
Eternity is now grown short;
A King is born without a court;
The water thirsts, the fountain's dry;
And life, being born, made apt to die.

G   81

Chorus.

Then let our praises emulate and vie
    With His humility!
Since He's exiled from skies
    That we might rise,—
From low estate of men
Let's sing Him up again!
Each man wind up his heart
To bear a part
In that angelic choir and show
His glory high as He was low.
Let's sing towards men good-will and charity,
Peace upon earth, glory to God on high!
              Hallelujah! Hallelujah!

JEREMY TAYLOR

46.   CHRISTMAS DAY

WONDER'S birthday,
    Which mak'st December's face
Fairer than May,
    And bidst the spring give place
To fresher winter, in whose hardy snow
A flower more sweet than the whole spring doth grow.

    For winter now
A virgin plant espies,
    Which all his snow
Could never equalize:
More white, more chaste is she, yet fertile too,
The King of Miracles would have it so.

Christmas Day

For he it was
Who would be born below,
And find a place
Amongst poor us to grow.
Himself he planted in our dust that he
Might be as true a mortal thing as we.

Himself he set
And by that art was sure
That he should get
A birth all clean and pure :
Proud flesh corrupts and stains the seed we sow ;
He, planted by his Spirit, will spotless grow.

Virginity
His Father wanteth not,
Though glorious he
So great a Son hath got ;
Wherefore Heaven orders that a virgin be
The Lily-Mother of his purity.

Upon the white
Church-wall oft-times have I
Observ'd the light,
Which darting from the sky
Pierc'd the unbroken glass and with it brought
The orient colours in the window wrought.

Christmas Day

So from his sphere
The Lord of Light doth come,
And passing here
His crystal Mother's womb
Leaves her entirely whole, yet brings away
Her perfect image, born a man to-day.

He who did wear
God's radiant boundless form
Shrinks himself here
Into a simple worm.
Heaven moulded up in earth ; Eternity
Grasp'd in a span of time doth bounded lie.

All Paradise
Collected in one bud
Doth sweetly rise
From its fair Virgin bed :
Omnipotence an Infant's shape puts on,
Immensity becomes a Little One.

But only Love
Would not thus scanted be,
But stoutly strove
'Gainst this conspiracy
Of strange Epitomies, and did display
Itself more full on this contracting day.

JOSEPH BEAUMONT

SONNET XXV

Incarnatio est maximum Dei donum.

LIKE as the fountain of all light created
   Doth pour out streams of brightness undefin'd
Through all the conduits of transparent kind,
That heaven and air are both illuminated,
And yet his light is not thereby abated;
So God's eternal bounty ever shin'd
The beams of being, moving, life, sense, mind;
And to all things himself communicated
But for the violent diffusive pleasure
Of goodness that left not till God had spent
Himself by giving us himself his treasure
In making man a God omnipotent.
How might this goodness draw ourselves above
Which drew down God with such attractive love!

JOSEPH BEAUMONT

48. ON THE NATIVITY OF OUR SAVIOUR

WHY does the frowning winter smile
   And check his fierce intent?
Why does he curb his ruffling powers,
As he for snow would sprinkle flowers?
There is a reason for this guile,
   'Twas but to pay his rent:
It is the best that Huff-capp gives
     At the great birth
     Of publicke mirth,
And pay'd, no longer lives.

On the Nativity of our Saviour

The Babe unveils His lovely face
   To chase the shades away;
As soon as He casts up His eyes
A sudden brightness will arise
To gild the room does Him embrace;
   In spite of clouds 'tis Day.
Lodg'd in His mother's bosom He
     May sleep in snow,
     (Without cold tho')
For down from cold is free.

Be not amazèd, souls, for this
   Is but the half of Joy;
The Angels spare their nimble wings,
For now they're but superfluous things;
To men, since Heaven descended is
   Contracted in a Boy.
The Rose of Sharon's budded now
     And every thing
     Portends a spring.
December snows adieu:

Adieu, but stay: a Subject prov'd a Ring,
Presents as great, as splendid, offering.
My breast's the mine whence golden precepts rise,
Myrrh drops in bitter tears from virgin eyes.
Frankincense, praise's furnish'd with desert
Offered upon no altar but my heart,
This reinvites my God unto my breast
And spreads the table for the welcome guest.

Tho' gold, myrrh, frankincense, kings off'red Thee,
Thou'st frankincense, with gold and myrrh from me.
If these shrink in performance, at Thy eyes
I'll trine my selfe and prove Thy sacrifice.

M. J.

49.   THE SHEPHERDS

SWEET, harmless live[r]s! on whose holy leisure,
Waits innocence and pleasure;
Whose leaders to those pastures and clear springs
    Were patriarchs, saints, and kings;
How happen'd it that in the dead of night
    You only saw true light,
While Palestine was fast asleep, and lay
    Without one thought of day?
Was it because those first and blessèd swains
    Were pilgrims on those plains
When they received the promise, for which now
    'Twas there first shown to you?
'Tis true he loves that dust whereon they go
    That serve him here below,
And therefore might for memory of those
    His love there first disclose;
But wretched Salem, once his love, must now
    No voice nor vision know;
Her stately piles with all their height and pride
    Now languishèd and died,

The Shepherds

And Bethlem's humble cots above them stept
  While all her seers slept;
Her cedar, fir, hewed stones, and gold were all
  Polluted through their fall;
And those once sacred mansions were now
  Mere emptiness and show.
This made the angel call at reeds and thatch,
  Yet where the shepherds watch,
And God's own lodging, though he could not lack,
  To be a common rack.
No costly pride, no soft-clothed luxury
  In those thin cells could lie;
Each stirring wind and storm blew through their cots,
  Which never harboured plots;
Only content and love and humble joys
  Lived there without all noise;
Perhaps some harmless cares for the next day
  Did in their bosoms play,
As where to lead their sheep, what silent nook,
  What springs or shades to look;
But that was all; and now with gladsome care
  They for the town prepare;
They leave their flock, and in a busy talk
  All towards Bethlem walk,
To seek their soul's great Shepherd, who was come
  To bring all stragglers home;
Where now they find Him out, and, taught before,
  That Lamb of God adore,
That Lamb, whose days great kings and prophets wished
  And longed to see, but missed.

88

The Shepherds

The first light they beheld was bright and gay,
    And turned their night to day ;
But to this later light they saw in Him
    Their day was dark and dim.

HENRY VAUGHAN

50.   CHRIST'S NATIVITY

AWAKE, glad heart ! get up and sing !
It is the Birthday of thy King.
    Awake ! awake !
    The sun doth shake
Light from his locks, and, all the way
Breathing perfumes, doth spice the day.

Awake ! awake ! hark how th' wood rings,
Winds whisper, and the busy springs
    A concert make !
    Awake ! awake !
Man is their high-priest, and should rise
To offer up the sacrifice.

I would I were some bird or star,
Fluttering in woods, or lifted far
    Above this inn,
    And road of sin !
Then either star or bird should be
Shining or singing still to Thee.

I would I had in my best part
Fit rooms for Thee ! or that my heart
    Were so clean as
    Thy manger was !
 But I am all filth, and obscene :
Yet, if Thou wilt, Thou canst make clean.

Sweet Jesu ! will then.   Let no more
This leper haunt and soil Thy door !
    Cure him, ease him,
    O release him !
And let once more, by mystic birth,
The Lord of life be born in earth.

HENRY VAUGHAN

51. AND THEY LAID HIM IN A MANGER

HAPPY crib, that wert alone
    To my God, bed, cradle, throne !
Whilst thy glorious vileness I
View with divine fancy's eye,
Sordid filth seems all the cost,
State, and splendour, crowns do boast.
See heaven's sacred majesty
Humbled beneath poverty ;
Swaddled up in homely rags,
On a bed of straw and flags !
He whose hands the heavens display'd,
And the world's foundations laid,

From the world almost exiled,
 Of all ornaments despoil'd.
 Perfumes bathe Him not, new-born,
Persian mantles not adorn;
 Nor do the rich roofs look bright,
With the jasper's orient light.
Where, O royal Infant, be
Th' ensigns of Thy majesty;
Thy Sire's equalizing state;
And Thy sceptre that rules fate?
Where's Thy angel-guarded throne,
Whence Thy laws Thou didst make known—
Laws which heaven, earth, hell, obey'd?
These, ah! these aside He laid;
Would the emblem be—of pride
By humility outvied?

SIR EDWARD SHERBURNE

52.   AT THE SIGN OF THE HEART

BUT art Thou come, dear Saviour? hath Thy love
Thus made Thee stoop, and leave Thy throne above

Thy lofty heavens, and thus Thyself to dress
In dust to visit mortals? Could no less

A condescension serve? and after all
The mean reception of a cratch and stall?

Dear Lord, I'll fetch Thee thence! I have a room
('Tis poor, but 'tis my best) if Thou wilt come

91

Within so small a cell, where I would fain
Mine and the world's Redeemer entertain,

I mean, my Heart: 'tis sluttish, I confess,
And will not mend Thy lodging, Lord, unless

Thou send before Thy harbinger, I mean
Thy pure and purging Grace, to make it clean

And sweep its nasty corners; then I'll try
To wash it also with a weeping eye.

And when 'tis swept and wash'd, I then will go
And, with Thy leave, I'll fetch some flowers that grow

In Thine own garden, Faith and Love, to Thee;
With these I'll dress it up, and these shall be

My rosemary and bays. Yet when my best
Is done, the room's not fit for such a Guest.

But here's the cure; Thy presence, Lord, alone
Will make a stall a Court, a cratch a Throne.

UNKNOWN

53.   LODGED IN AN INN

LODGED in an inn
What Guest divine
There meekly lay,
The God of night and day!
In tax-time to pay sums
    He comes,

Ev'n man's price full:
From Satan's rule
He will set free
Our poor humanity.

To us betake
Blest God! and make
Within our breast
Thy lodging-place and rest;
Thou Temples seek'st, not Inns:
Let sins
No more intrude
On th' Inmate God,
Nor e'er deface
The ornaments of grace.

UNKNOWN

54. YET IF HIS MAJESTY OUR SOVEREIGN LORD

YET if his majesty our sovereign Lord
Should of his own accord
Friendly himself invite,
And say, 'I'll be your guest to-morrow night,'
How should we stir ourselves, call and command
All hands to work! 'Let no man idle stand.

'Set me fine Spanish tables in the hall,
See they be fitted all;
Let there be room to eat,
And order taken that there want no meat.
See every sconce and candlestick made bright,
That without tapers they may give a light.

' Look to the presence : are the carpets spread,
The daïs o'er the head,
The cushions in the chairs,
And all the candles lighted on the stairs ?
Perfume the chambers, and in any case
Let each man give attendance in his place.'

Thus if the king were coming would we do,
And 'twere good reason too ;
For 'tis a duteous thing
To show all honour to an earthly king,
And after all our travail and our cost,
So he be pleased, to think no labour lost.

But at the coming of the King of heaven,
All 's set at six and seven.
We wallow in our sin,
Christ cannot find a chamber in the inn,
We entertain Him always like a stranger,
And as at first still lodge Him in the manger.

UNKNOWN

55.   AND ART THOU COME, BLEST BABE?

AND art Thou come, blest Babe, and come to me ?
Come down to teach me how to come to Thee ?
Welcome, thrice welcome to my panting soul,
Which, as it loves, doth grieve that 'tis so foul.

The less 'tis fit for Thee come from above,
The more it needs Thee, and the more I love.

UNKNOWN

56.   SONG OF THE ANGELS AT THE NATIVITY

WHILE shepherds watch'd their flocks by night,
   All seated on the ground,
The Angel of the Lord came down,
   And glory shone around.

'Fear not,' said he (for mighty dread
   Had seized their troubled mind);
'Glad tidings of great joy I bring
   To you and all mankind.

'To you in David's town this day
   Is born of David's line
The Saviour, who is Christ the Lord;
   And this shall be the sign:—

'The heavenly Babe you there shall find
   To human view display'd,
All meanly wrapt in swathing-bands,
   And in a manger laid.'

Thus spake the seraph; and forthwith
   Appear'd a shining throng
Of angels praising God, and thus
   Address'd their joyful song:—

'All glory be to God on high,
   And to the earth be peace;
Good-will henceforth from heaven to men
   Begin, and never cease!'

NAHUM TATE

95

SHEPHERDS, rejoice, lift up your eyes,
  And send your fears away;
News from the region of the skies!
  Salvation's born to-day.

'Jesus, the God whom angels fear,
  Comes down to dwell with you;
To-day He makes His entrance here,
  But not as monarchs do.

'No gold, nor purple swaddling-bands,
  Nor royal shining things;
A manger for His cradle stands
  And holds the King of kings.

'Go, shepherds, where the Infant lies,
  And see His humble throne:—
With tears of joy in all your eyes
  Go, shepherds, kiss the Son.'

Thus Gabriel sang: and straight around
  The heavenly armies throng;
They tune their harps to lofty sound,
  And thus conclude the song:

'Glory to God that reigns above,
  Let peace surround the earth;
Mortals shall know their Maker's love,
  At their Redeemer's birth.'

Lord! and shall angels have their songs,
    And men no tunes to raise?
O may we lose these useless tongues
    When they forget to praise!

Glory to God that reigns above,
    That pitied us forlorn!
We join to sing our Maker's love—
    For there's a Saviour born.

ISAAC WATTS

58.   A CRADLE SONG

HUSH, my dear, lie still and slumber,
    Holy angels guard thy bed!
Heavenly blessings without number
    Gently falling on thy head.

Sleep, my babe; thy food and raiment,
    House and home thy friends provide;
All without thy care or payment,
    All thy wants are well supplied.

How much better thou'rt attended
    Than the Son of God could be,
When from heaven He descended,
    And became a Child like thee!

Soft and easy is thy cradle;
    Coarse and hard thy Saviour lay:
When His birthplace was a stable,
    And His softest bed was hay.

H

See the kinder shepherds round Him,
    Telling wonders from the sky!
Where they sought Him, there they found Him,
    With the virgin-mother by.

See the lovely Babe a-dressing;
    Lovely Infant, how He smiled!
When He wept, the mother's blessing
    Soothed and hushed the holy Child.

Lo, He slumbers in His manger
    Where the hornèd oxen fed;
—Peace, my darling, here's no danger;
    Here's no ox a-near thy bed.

Mayst thou live to know and fear Him,
    Trust and love Him all thy days;
Then go dwell for ever near Him,
    See His face, and sing His praise.

I could give thee thousand kisses,
    Hoping what I most desire;
Not a mother's fondest wishes
    Can to greater joys aspire.

ISAAC WATTS

59. A HYMN FOR CHRISTMAS DAY

CHRISTIANS, awake, salute the happy morn
    Whereon the Saviour of the world was born;
Rise to adore the Mystery of love,
Which hosts of angels chanted from above:

With them the joyful tidings first begun
Of God incarnate, and the Virgin's Son:
Then to the watchful shepherds it was told,
Who heard th' Angelic Herald's voice—' Behold!
I bring good tidings of a Saviour's birth
To you, and all the nations upon earth;
This day hath God fulfill'd his promised word;
This day is born a Saviour, Christ, the Lord:
In David's city, shepherds, ye shall find
The long-foretold Redeemer of mankind,
Wrapt up in swaddling-clothes, the Babe divine
Lies in a manger; this shall be the sign.'

JOHN BYROM

60. A HYMN FOR CHRISTMAS DAY

HARK, the glad sound! the Saviour comes,
The Saviour promised long;
Let every heart prepare a throne,
And every voice a song!

He comes, the prisoners to release
In Satan's bondage held;
The gates of brass before Him burst,
The iron fetters yield.

He comes, the broken heart to bind,
The bleeding soul to cure,
And with the treasures of His grace
T' enrich the humble poor.

A Hymn for Christmas Day

Our glad Hosannas, Prince of Peace,
    Thy welcome shall proclaim,
And heaven's eternal arches ring
    With Thy belovèd name.

PHILIP DODDRIDGE

61.   A HYMN FOR CHRISTMAS DAY

HARK! how all the welkin rings,
    Glory to the King of kings!
Peace on earth, and mercy mild,
God and sinners reconciled!
Joyful, all ye nations, rise,
Join the triumph of the skies;
Universal nature say,
Christ the Lord is born to-day.

Christ, by highest Heaven adored;
Christ, the Everlasting Lord;
Late in time behold Him come,
Offspring of a Virgin's womb;
Veil'd in flesh the Godhead see;
Hail, th' Incarnate Deity!
Pleased as man with men t' appear,
Jesus, our Immanuel here!

Hail! the heavenly Prince of Peace!
Hail! the Sun of Righteousness!
Light and life to all He brings,
Risen with healing in His wings.

A Hymn for Christmas Day

Mild He lays His glory by,
Born that man no more may die,
Born to raise the sons of earth,
Born to give them second birth.

CHARLES WESLEY

62. THE SHEPHERDS WENT THEIR HASTY WAY

THE shepherds went their hasty way,
    And found the lowly stable-shed,
Where the virgin-mother lay;
    And now they checked their eager tread,
For to the Babe, that at her bosom clung,
A mother's song the virgin-mother sung.

They told her how a glorious light,
    Streaming from a heavenly throng,
Around them shone, suspending night!
    While sweeter than a mother's song,
Blest angels heralded the Saviour's birth,
Glory to God on high! and peace on earth!

She listened to the tale divine,
    And closer still the Babe she pressed;
And while she cried, The Babe is mine!
    The milk rushed faster to her breast:
Joy rose within her, like a summer's morn;
Peace, peace on earth! the Prince of Peace is born.

The Shepherds went their Hasty Way

Thou mother of the Prince of Peace,
   Poor, simple, and of low estate!
That strife should vanish, battle cease,
   O why should this thy soul elate?
Sweet music's loudest note, the poet's story,—
Didst thou ne'er love to hear of fame and glory?

And is not War a youthful king,
   A stately hero clad in mail?
Beneath his footsteps laurels spring;
   Him earth's majestic monarchs hail
Their friend, their playmate! and his bold bright eye
Compels the maiden's love-confessing sigh.

'Tell this in some more courtly scene
   To maids and youths in robes of state!
I am a woman poor and mean,
   And therefore is my soul elate.
War is a ruffian, all with guilt defiled,
That from the aged father tears his child.

'A murderous fiend by fiends adored,
   He kills the sire and starves the son;
The husband kills, and from her board
   Steals all his widow's toil had won;
Plunders God's world of beauty; rends away
All safety from the night, all comfort from the day.

'Then wisely is my soul elate,
    That strife should vanish, battle cease;
I'm poor and of a low estate,
    The mother of the Prince of Peace.
Joy rises in me, like a summer's morn:
Peace, peace on earth! the Prince of Peace is born.'

SAMUEL TAYLOR COLERIDGE

63. FROM OTTFRIED'S PARAPHRASE OF THE GOSPEL

SHE gave with joy her virgin breast;
    She hid it not, she bared the breast
Which suckled that divinest Babe!
Blessed, blessed were the breasts
Which the Saviour Infant kiss'd;
And blessed, blessed was the mother
Who wrapp'd His limbs in swaddling clothes,
Singing placed Him on her lap,
Hung o'er Him with her looks of love,
And soothed Him with a lulling motion.
Blessed! for she shelter'd Him
From the damp and chilling air;
Blessed, blessed! for she lay
With such a Babe in one blest bed,
Close as babes and mothers lie!
Blessed, blessed evermore,
With her virgin lips she kiss'd,

With her arms, and to her breast,
She embraced the Babe divine,
Her Babe divine the virgin-mother!
There lives not on this ring of earth
A mortal that can sing her praise.
Mighty mother, virgin pure,
In the darkness and the night
For us she *bore* the heavenly Lord.

SAMUEL TAYLOR COLERIDGE

64.   THE VIRGIN'S CRADLE HYMN

Copied from a print of the Virgin in a Catholic village in Germany.

DORMI, Jesu! mater ridet
Quae tam dulcem somnum videt,
   Dormi, Jesu! blandule!
Si non dormis, mater plorat,
Inter fila cantans orat,
   Blande, veni, somnule.

Sleep, sweet babe! my cares beguiling:
Mother sits beside thee smiling;
   Sleep, my darling, tenderly;
If thou sleep not, mother mourneth,
Singing as her wheel she turneth:
   Come, soft slumber, balmily!

SAMUEL TAYLOR COLERIDGE

65. BRIGHTEST AND BEST OF THE SONS OF THE MORNING!

BRIGHTEST and best of the sons of the morning!
Dawn on our darkness, and lend us thine aid!
Star of the East, the horizon adorning,
   Guide where our Infant Redeemer is laid!

Cold on His cradle the dew-drops are shining;
   Low lies His head with the beasts of the stall;
Angels adore Him, in slumber reclining,
   Maker and Monarch and Saviour of all.

Say, shall we yield Him, in costly devotion,
   Odours of Edom and offerings divine?
Gems of the mountain, and pearls of the ocean,
   Myrrh from the forest, or gold from the mine?

Vainly we offer each ample oblation;
   Vainly with gifts would His favour secure;
Richer by far is the heart's adoration;
   Dearer to God are the prayers of the poor.

Brightest and best of the sons of the morning!
   Dawn on our darkness, and lend us thine aid!
Star of the East, the horizon adorning,
   Guide where our Infant Redeemer is laid!

REGINALD HEBER

66. THEY LEAVE THE LAND OF GEMS AND GOLD

THEY leave the land of gems and gold,
　　The shining portals of the East;
For Him, the woman's Seed foretold,
　　They leave the revel and the feast.

To earth their sceptres they have cast,
　　And crowns by kings ancestral worn;
They track the lonely Syrian waste;
　　They kneel before the Babe new born.

O happy eyes that saw Him first;
　　O happy lips that kissed His feet;
Earth slakes at last her ancient thirst;
　　With Eden's joy her pulses beat.

True kings are those who thus forsake
　　Their kingdoms for the Eternal King;
Serpent, her foot is on thy neck;
　　Herod, thou writhest, but canst not sting.

He, He is King, and He alone
　　Who lifts that infant hand to bless;
Who makes His mother's knee His throne,
　　Yet rules the starry wilderness.

AUBREY DE VERE

1

THE time draws near the birth of Christ:
The moon is hid; the night is still;
The Christmas bells from hill to hill
Answer each other in the mist.

Four voices of four hamlets round,
From far and near, on mead and moor,
Swell out and fail, as if a door
Were shut between me and the sound:

Each voice four changes on the wind,
That now dilate, and now decrease,
Peace and goodwill, goodwill and peace,
Peace and goodwill, to all mankind.

This year I slept and woke with pain,
I almost wish'd no more to wake,
And that my hold on life would break
Before I heard those bells again:

But they my troubled spirit rule,
For they controll'd me when a boy;
They bring me sorrow touch'd with joy,
The merry, merry bells of Yule.

2

Ring out, wild bells, to the wild sky,
The flying cloud, the frosty light:
The year is dying in the night;
Ring out, wild bells, and let him die.

Christmas and New Year Bells

Ring out the old, ring in the new,
    Ring, happy bells, across the snow:
    The year is going, let him go;
Ring out the false, ring in the true.

Ring out the grief that saps the mind,
    For these that here we see no more;
    Ring out the feud of rich and poor,
Ring in redress to all mankind.

Ring out a slowly dying cause,
    And ancient forms of party strife;
    Ring in the nobler modes of life,
With sweeter manners, purer laws.

Ring out the want, the care, the sin,
    The faithless coldness of the times;
    Ring out, ring out my mournful rhymes,
But ring the fuller minstrel in.

Ring out false pride in place and blood,
    The civic slander and the spite;
    Ring in the love of truth and right,
Ring in the common love of good.

Ring out old shapes of foul disease;
    Ring out the narrowing lust of gold;
    Ring out the thousand wars of old,
Ring in the thousand years of peace.

Ring in the valiant man and free,
    The larger heart, the kindlier hand;
    Ring out the darkness of the land,
Ring in the Christ that is to be.

ALFRED TENNYSON (from *In Memoriam*)

THE FIRST CHRISTMAS EVE

IT was the calm and silent night:
  Seven hundred years and fifty-three
Had Rome been growing up to might,
  And now was Queen of earth and sea :
The clashing of continual wars
  Was hushed throughout the wide domain;
Apollo, Pallas, Jove and Mars
  Held undisturbed their ancient reign,
    In the solemn midnight
      Centuries ago.

It was the calm and silent night:
  The Senator of ancient Rome
Impatient urged his chariot's flight,
  From lordly revel rolling home :
Triumphal arches gleaming swell
  His breast with thoughts of boundless sway;
Nought recked the Roman what befell
  A paltry province far away,
    In the solemn midnight
      Centuries ago.

Within that province far away,
  Went plodding home the weary boor.
A streak of light before him lay,
  Fallen through a half-shut stable door

The First Christmas Eve

Across his path :—he passed ; for nought
  Told what was going on within ;
How bright the stars his only thought,
  The air, how calm and cold and thin
    In the solemn midnight
      Centuries ago.

Oh strange indifference ! low and high
  Drowsed over common joys and cares—
The earth was still, it knew not why,
  The world was listening unawares,
How calm a moment may precede
  One that shall thrill the world for ever.
To that still moment none would heed,
  Man's doom was linked, no more to sever,
    In the solemn midnight
      Centuries ago.

It is the calm and silent night—
  A thousand bells ring out, and throw
Their joyous peals around, and smite
  The darkness—charmed and holy now—
The day that erst no name had worn,
  To it a blessed name is given,
For in that stable lay, new born,
  The Peaceful Prince of earth and heaven—
    In the solemn midnight
      Centuries ago.

ALFRED DOMETT

69. CHRIST WAS BORN ON CHRISTMAS DAY

CHRIST was born on Christmas day ;
Wreathe the holly, twine the bay ;
 Christus natus hodie:
The Babe, the Son, the Holy One of Mary.

He is born to set us free,
He is born our Lord to be,
 Ex Maria Virgine:
The God, the Lord, by all adored for ever.

Let the bright red berries glow
Everywhere in goodly show ;
 Christus natus hodie:
The Babe, the Son, the Holy One of Mary.

Christian men, rejoice and sing ;
'Tis the birthday of a King,
 Ex Maria Virgine :
The God, the Lord, by all adored for ever.

Night of sadness, Morn of gladness
   Evermore :
Ever, ever, after many troubles sore,
Morn of gladness, evermore and evermore.

Midnight scarcely passed and over,
Drawing to this holy morn,
Very early, very early
Christ was born.

Sing out with bliss, His name is this—
    Emmanuel,
As was foretold in days of old
    By Gabriel.

J. M. NEALE

70.   A CHRISTMAS CAROL

IT chanced upon the merry merry Christmas eve
  I went sighing past the church across the moorland
    dreary—
' Oh! never sin and want and woe this earth will leave,
  And the bells but mock the wailing round, they sing
    so cheery.
How long, O Lord! how long before Thou come again?
  Still in cellar, and in garret, and on moorland dreary
The orphans moan, and widows weep, and poor men
    toil in vain,
  Till earth is sick of hope deferred, though Christmas
    bells be cheery.'

Then arose a joyous clamour from the wildfowl on the
    mere,
  Beneath the stars, across the snow, like clear bells
    ringing,
And a voice within cried—' Listen!—Christmas carols
    even here!
  Though thou be dumb, yet o'er their work the stars
    and snows are singing.

Blind! I live, I love, I reign; and all the nations
 through
 With the thunder of my judgements even now are
  ringing;
Do thou fulfil thy work, but as yon wildfowl do,
 Thou wilt hear no less the wailing, yet hear through
  it angels singing.'

        CHARLES KINGSLEY

71.   A CHRISTMAS CAROL

IN the bleak mid-winter
 Frosty wind made moan,
Earth stood hard as iron,
 Water like a stone;
Snow had fallen, snow on snow,
 Snow on snow,
In the bleak mid-winter
 Long ago.

Our God, heaven cannot hold Him,
 Nor earth sustain;
Heaven and earth shall flee away
 When He comes to reign:
In the bleak mid-winter
 A stable-place sufficed
The Lord God Almighty
 Jesus Christ.

I   113

A Christmas Carol

Enough for Him whom cherubim
  Worship night and day,
A breastful of milk
  And a mangerful of hay;
Enough for Him whom angels
  Fall down before,
The ox and ass and camel
  Which adore.

Angels and archangels
  May have gathered there,
Cherubim and seraphim
  Thronged the air:
But only His mother,
  In her maiden bliss,
Worshipped the Belovèd
  With a kiss.

What can I give Him,
  Poor as I am?
If I were a shepherd
  I would bring a lamb,
If I were a wise man
  I would do my part,—
Yet what I can I give Him:
  Give my heart.

CHRISTINA ROSSETTI

To Bethlem did they go, the shepherds three;
To Bethlem did they go, to see whe'r it were so or no,
    Whether Christ were born or no
      To set men free.

    Masters, in this hall,
      Hear ye news to-day
    Brought over sea,
      And ever I you pray,
        Nowell! Nowell! Nowell! Nowell!
          Sing we clear!
        Holpen are all folk on earth,
          Born is God's Son so dear.

    Going over the hills
      Through the milk-white snow,
    Heard I ewes bleat
      While the wind did blow.
        Nowell, &c.

    Shepherds many an one
      Sat among the sheep;
    No man spake more word
      Than they had been asleep.
        Nowell, &c.

    Quoth I, 'Fellows mine,
      Why this guise sit ye?
    Making but dull cheer,
      Shepherds though ye be?'
        Nowell, &c.

'Shepherds should of right
  Leap and dance and sing;
Thus to see ye sit
  Is a right strange thing.'
    Nowell, &c.

Quoth these fellows then,
  'To Bethlem town we go,
To see a mighty Lord
  Lie in manger low.'
    Nowell, &c.

'How name ye this Lord,
  Shepherds?' then said I.
'Very God,' they said,
  'Come from heaven high.'
    Nowell, &c.

Then to Bethlem town
  We went two and two,
And in a sorry place
  Heard the oxen low.
    Nowell, &c.

Therein did we see
  A sweet and goodly May,
And a fair old man;
  Upon the straw she lay.
    Nowell, &c.

And a little Child
  On her arm had she;
' Wot ye who This is? '
  Said the hinds to me.
    Nowell, &c.

Ox and ass Him know,
  Kneeling on their knee:
Wondrous joy had I
  This little Babe to see.
    Nowell, &c.

This is Christ the Lord,
  Masters, be ye glad!
Christmas is come in,
  And no folk should be sad.
    Nowell, &c.

WILLIAM MORRIS

73. OUTLANDERS, WHENCE COME YE LAST?

OUTLANDERS, whence come ye last?
  The snow in the street and the wind on the door.
Through what green sea and great have ye passed?
  Minstrels and maids, stand forth on the floor.

From far away, O masters mine,
  The snow in the street and the wind on the door.
We come to bear you goodly wine:
  Minstrels and maids, stand forth on the floor.

Outlanders, whence come ye last?

From far away we come to you,
  The snow in the street and the wind on the door.
To tell of great tidings strange and true:
  Minstrels and maids, stand forth on the floor.

News, news of the Trinity,
  The snow in the street and the wind on the door.
And Mary and Joseph from over the sea:
  Minstrels and maids, stand forth on the floor.

For as we wandered far and wide,
  The snow in the street and the wind on the door.
What hap do ye deem there should us betide?
  Minstrels and maids, stand forth on the floor.

Under a bent when the night was deep,
  The snow in the street and the wind on the door.
There lay three shepherds tending their sheep:
  Minstrels and maids, stand forth on the floor.

' O ye shepherds, what have ye seen,
  The snow in the street and the wind on the door,
To slay your sorrow and heal your teen?'
  Minstrels and maids, stand forth on the floor.

' In an ox-stall this night we saw,
  The snow in the street and the wind on the door,
A Babe and a maid without a flaw.'
  Minstrels and maids, stand forth on the floor.

'There was an old man there beside,
   The snow in the street and the wind on the door,
His hair was white and his hood was wide.'
   Minstrels and maids, stand forth on the floor.

'And as we gazed this thing upon,
   The snow in the street and the wind on the door,
Those twain knelt down to the Little One.'
   Minstrels and maids, stand forth on the floor.

'And a marvellous song we straight did hear,
   The snow in the street and the wind on the door,
That slew our sorrow and healed our care.'
   Minstrels and maids, stand forth on the floor.

News of a fair and a marvellous thing,
   The snow in the street and the wind on the door.
Nowell, nowell, nowell, we sing!
   Minstrels and maids, stand forth on the floor.

WILLIAM MORRIS

74. SIR GALAHAD, A CHRISTMAS MYSTERY

IT is the longest night in all the year,
   Near on the day when the Lord Christ was born;
Six hours ago I came and sat down here,
   And ponder'd sadly, wearied and forlorn.

Sir Galahad, A Christmas Mystery

The winter wind that pass'd the chapel door,
    Sang out a moody tune, that went right well
With mine own thoughts : I look'd down on the floor,
    Between my feet, until I heard a bell

Sound a long way off through the forest deep,
    And toll on steadily ; a drowsiness
Came on me, so that I fell half asleep,
    As I sat there not moving : less and less

I saw the melted snow that hung in beads
    Upon my steel shoes ; less and less I saw
Between the tiles the bunches of small weeds :
    Heartless and stupid, with no touch of awe

Upon me, half-shut eyes upon the ground,
    I thought ; O Galahad ! the days go by,
Stop and cast up now that which you have found,
    So sorely you have wrought and painfully.

Night after night your horse treads down alone
    The sere damp fern, night after night you sit
Holding the bridle like a man of stone,
    Dismal, unfriended, what thing comes of it.

And what if Palomydes also ride,
    And over many a mountain and bare heath
Follow the questing beast with none beside ?
    Is he not able still to hold his breath

With thoughts of Iseult? doth he not grow pale
   With weary striving, to seem best of all
To her, ' as she is best,' he saith? to fail
   Is nothing to him, he can never fall.

For unto such a man love-sorrow is
   So dear a thing unto his constant heart,
That even if he never win one kiss,
   Or touch from Iseult, it will never part.

And he will never know her to be worse
   Than in his happiest dreams he thinks she is:
Good knight, and faithful, you have 'scaped the curse
   In wonderful-wise; you have great store of bliss.

Yea, what if Father Launcelot ride out,
   Can he not think of Guenevere's arms, round,
Warm and lithe, about his neck, and shout
   Till all the place grows joyful with the sound?

And when he lists can often see her face,
   And think, ' Next month I kiss you, or next week,
And still you think of me ': therefore the place
   Grows very pleasant, whatsoever he seek.

But me, who ride alone, some carle shall find
   Dead in my arms in the half-melted snow,
When all unkindly with the shifting wind,
   The thaw comes on at Candlemas: I know

Indeed that they will say: ' This Galahad
  If he had lived had been a right good knight;
Ah! poor chaste body!' but they will be glad,
  Not most alone, but all, when in their sight

That very evening in their scarlet sleeves
  The gay-dress'd minstrels sing; no maid will talk
Of sitting on my tomb, until the leaves,
  Grown big upon the bushes of the walk,

East of the Palace-pleasaunce, make it hard
  To see the minster therefrom: well-a-day!
Before the trees by autumn were well bared,
  I saw a damozel with gentle play,

Within that very walk say last farewell
  To her dear knight, just riding out to find
(Why should I choke to say it?) the Sangreal,
  And their last kisses sunk into my mind,

Yea, for she stood lean'd forward on his breast,
  Rather, scarce stood; the back of one dear hand,
That it might well be kiss'd, she held and press'd
  Against his lips; long time they stood there, fann'd

By gentle gusts of quiet frosty wind,
  Till Mador de la Porte a-going by,
And my own horsehoofs roused them; they untwined,
  And parted like a dream.   In this way I,

Sir Galahad, A Christmas Mystery

With sleeply face bent to the chapel floor,
  Kept musing half asleep, till suddenly
A sharp bell rang from close beside the door,
  And I leapt up when something pass'd me by,

Shrill ringing going with it, still half blind
  I stagger'd after, a great sense of awe
At every step kept gathering on my mind,
  Thereat I have no marvel, for I saw

One sitting on the altar as a throne,
  Whose face no man could say he did not know,
And though the bell still rang, he sat alone,
  With raiment half blood-red, half white as snow.

Right so I fell upon the floor and knelt,
  Not as one kneels in church when mass is said,
But in a heap, quite nerveless, for I felt
  The first time what a thing was perfect dread.

But mightily the gentle voice came down:
  ' Rise up, and look and listen, Galahad,
Good knight of God, for you will see no frown
  Upon my face; I came to make you glad.

' For that you say that you are all alone,
  I will be with you always, and fear not
You are uncared for, though no maiden moan
  Above your empty tomb; for Launcelot,

'He in good time shall be my servant too,
  Meantime, take note whose sword first made him
    knight,
And who has loved him alway, yea, and who
  Still trusts him alway, though in all men's sight,

'He is just what you know, O Galahad,
  This love is happy even as you say,
But would you for a little time be glad,
  To make ME sorry long day after day?

'Her warm arms round his neck half throttle Me,
  The hot love-tears burn deep like spots of lead,
Yea, and the years pass quick: right dismally
  Will Launcelot at one time hang his head;

'Yea, old and shrivell'd he shall win my love.
  Poor Palomydes fretting out his soul!
Not always is he able, son, to move
  His love, and do it honour: needs must roll

'The proudest destrier sometimes in the dust,
  And then 'tis weary work; he strives beside
Seem better than he is, so that his trust
  Is always on what chances may betide;

'And so he wears away, my servant, too,
  When all these things are gone, and wretchedly
He sits and longs to moan for Iseult, who
  Is no care now to Palomydes: see,

Sir Galahad, A Christmas Mystery

‘ O good son Galahad, upon this day,
   Now even, all these things are on your side,
But these you fight not for ; look up, I say,
   And see how I can love you, for no pride

‘ Closes your eyes, no vain lust keeps them down.
   See now you have ME always ; following
That holy vision, Galahad, go on,
   Until at last you come to Me to sing

‘ In heaven always, and to walk around
   The garden where I am ’ : he ceased, my face
And wretched body fell upon the ground ;
   And when I look’d again, the holy place

Was empty ; but right so the bell again
   Came to the chapel-door, there entered
Two angels first, in white, without a stain,
   And scarlet wings, then after them a bed,

Four ladies bore, and set it down beneath
   The very altar-step, and while for fear
I scarcely dared to move or draw my breath,
   Those holy ladies gently came a-near,

And quite unarm’d me, saying : ‘ Galahad,
   Rest here a while and sleep, and take no thought
Of any other thing than being glad ;
   Hither the Sangreal will be shortly brought,

Sir Galahad, A Christmas Mystery

' Yet must you sleep the while it stayeth here.'
    Right so they went away, and I, being weary,
Slept long and dream'd of heaven: the bell comes near,
    I doubt it grows to morning.   Miserere!

[*Enter two angels in white, with scarlet wings; also, four
    ladies in gowns of red and green; also an angel, bearing
    in his hands a surcoat of white, with a red cross.*]

An Angel.
    O servant of the high God, Galahad!
        Rise and be arm'd, the Sangreal is gone forth
    Through the great forest, and you must be had
        Unto the sea that lieth on the north:

    There shall you find the wondrous ship wherein
        The spindles of King Solomon are laid,
    And the sword that no man draweth without sin,
        But if he be most pure: and there is stay'd,

    Hard by, Sir Launcelot, whom you will meet
        In some short space upon that ship: first, though,
    Will come here presently that lady sweet,
        Sister of Percival, whom you well know,

    And with her Bors and Percival: stand now,
        These ladies will to arm you.

First Lady [*putting on the hauberke*].

                                    Galahad,
    That I may stand so close beneath your brow,
        I, Margaret of Antioch, am glad.

Sir Galahad, A Christmas Mystery

Second Lady [*girding him with the sword*].
 That I may stand and touch you with my hand,
  O Galahad, I, Cecily, am glad.

Third Lady [*buckling on the spurs*].
 That I may kneel while up above you stand,
  And gaze at me, O holy Galahad,

 I, Lucy, am most glad.

Fourth Lady [*putting on the basnet*].
     O gentle knight,
 That you bow down to us in reverence,
 We are most glad, I, Katherine, with delight
  Must needs fall trembling.

Angel [*putting on the crossed surcoat*].
     Galahad, we go hence,

 For here, amid the straying of the snow,
  Come Percival's sister, Bors, and Percival.
[*The four Ladies carry out the bed, and all go but Galahad.*]

Galahad.
 How still and quiet everything seems now !
  They come, too, for I hear the horsehoofs fall.

 [*Enter Sir Bors, Sir Percival, and his Sister.*]
 Fair friends and gentle lady, God you save !
  A many marvels have been here to-night ;
 Tell me what news of Launcelot you have,
  And has God's body ever been in sight ?

127

Sir Bors.

Why, as for seeing that same holy thing,
    As we were riding slowly side by side,
An hour ago, we heard a sweet voice sing,
    And through the bare twigs saw a great light glide,

With many-colour'd raiment, but far off,
    And so pass'd quickly—from the court nought good ;
Poor merry Dinadan, that with jape and scoff
    Kept us all merry, in a little wood

Was found all hack'd and dead ; Sir Lionel
    And Gauwaine have come back from the great
        quest,
Just merely shamed ; and Lauvaine, who loved well
    Your father Launcelot, at the king's behest

Went out to seek him, but was almost slain,
    Perhaps is dead now ; everywhere
The knights come foil'd from the great quest ; in vain,
    In vain they struggle for the vision fair.

WILLIAM MORRIS

75.   AISHAH SCHECHINAH

A SHAPE, like folded light, embodied air,
    Yet wreath'd with flesh and warm ;
All that of heaven is feminine and fair,
    Moulded in visible form.

Aishah Schechinah

She stood, the Lady Schechinah of earth,
    A chancel for the sky;
Where woke, to breath and beauty, God's own birth,
    For men to see Him by.

Round her, too pure to mingle with the day,
    Light, that was life, abode;
Folded within her fibres meekly lay
    The link of boundless God.

So link'd, so blent, that when, with pulse fulfill'd,
    Moved but that infant hand,
Far, far away, His conscious Godhead thrill'd,
    And stars might understand.

Lo! where they pause, with intergathering rest,
    The Threefold and the One!
And lo! He binds them to her orient breast,
    His Manhood girded on.

The Zone, where two glad worlds for ever meet,
    Beneath that bosom ran:
Deep in that womb, the conquering Paraclete
    Smote Godhead on to man!

Sole scene among the stars, where, yearning, glide
    The Threefold and the One:
Her God upon her lap, the Virgin-Bride,
    Her Awful Child, her Son.

R. S. Hawker

The Rubric

When the brown bowl is filled for yule, let the dome or upper half be set on; then let the waes-haelers kneel one by one and draw up the wine with their reeds through the two bosses at the rim. Let one breath only be drawn by each of the morice for his waes-hael.

WAES-HAEL for knight and dame!
O! merry be their dole;
Drink-hael! in Jesu's name
We fill the tawny bowl;
But cover down the curving crest,
Mould of the Orient Lady's breast.

Waes-hael! yet lift no lid:
Drain ye the reeds for wine.
Drink-hael! the milk was hid
That soothed that Babe divine;
Hushed, as this hollow channel flows,
He drew the balsam from the rose.

Waes-hael! thus glowed the breast
Where a God yearned to cling;
Drink-hael! so Jesu pressed
Life from its mystic spring;
Then hush, and bend in reverent sign,
And breathe the thrilling reeds for wine.

Waes-hael! in shadowy scene,
   Lo! Christmas children we;
Drink-hael! behold we lean
   At a far Mother's knee;
To dream, that thus her bosom smiled,
And learn the lip of Bethlehem's Child.

R. S. HAWKER

77.   REGINA COELI

SAY, did his Sisters wonder what could Joseph see
In a mild, silent little Maid like thee?
And was it awful, in that narrow house,
With God for Babe and Spouse?
Nay, like thy simple, female sort, each one
Apt to find Him in Husband and in Son,
Nothing to thee came strange in this.
Thy wonder was but wondrous bliss:
Wondrous, for, though
True Virgin lives not but does know,
(Howbeit none ever yet confess'd,)
That God lies really in her breast,
Of thine He made His special nest!
And so
All mothers worship little feet,
And kiss the very ground they've trod;
But, ah, thy little Baby sweet
Who was indeed thy God.

COVENTRY PATMORE

78. MARY MOTHER OF DIVINE GRACE, COMPARED TO THE AIR WE BREATHE

WILD air, world-mothering air,
　　Nestling me everywhere,
That each eyelash or hair
Girdles; goes home betwixt
The fleeciest, frailest-flixed
Snow-flake; that's fairly mixed
With, riddles, and is rife
In every least thing's life;
This needful, never spent
And nursing element;
My more than meat and drink,
My meal at every wink;
This air, which, by life's law,
My lung must draw and draw
Now, but to breathe its praise,—
Minds me in many ways
Of her who not only
Gave God's infinity,
Dwindled to infancy,
Welcome in womb and breast,
Birth, milk, and all the rest,
But mothers each new grace
That does now reach our race,
Mary Immaculate,
Merely a woman, yet
Whose presence, power is
Great as no goddess's

Mary Mother of Divine Grace

Was deemèd, dreamèd; who
This one work has to do—
Let all God's glory through,
God's glory, which would go
Through her and from her flow
Off, and no way but so.

I say that we are wound
With mercy round and round
As if with air: the same
Is Mary, more by name,
She, wild web, wondrous robe,
Mantles the guilty globe,
Since God has let dispense
Her prayers His providence.
Nay, more than almoner,
The sweet alms' self is her
And men are meant to share
Her life as life does air.

If I have understood,
She holds high motherhood
Towards all our ghostly good
And plays in grace her part
About man's beating heart,
Laying, like air's fine flood,
The death-dance in his blood;
Yet no part but what will
Be Christ our Saviour still.
Of her flesh he took flesh:
He does take, fresh and fresh,
Though much the mystery how,
Not flesh but spirit now

And wakes, O marvellous !
New Nazareths in us,
Where she shall yet conceive
Him, morning, noon, and eve;
New Bethlems, and he born
There, evening, noon and morn—
Bethlem or Nazareth,
Men here may draw like breath
More Christ, and baffle death;
Who, born so, comes to be
New self, and nobler me
In each one, and each one
More makes, when all is done,
Both God's and Mary's son.

   Again, look overhead
How air is azurèd.
O how ! nay do but stand
Where you can lift your hand
Skywards: rich, rich it laps
Round the four finger-gaps.
Yet such a sapphire-shot,
Charged, steepèd sky will not
Stain light.   Yea, mark you this:
It does no prejudice.
The glass-blue days are those
When every colour glows,
Each shape and shadow shows.
Blue be it: this blue heaven
The seven or seven times seven

Mary Mother of Divine Grace

Hued sunbeam will transmit
Perfect, not alter it.
Or if there does some soft
On things aloof, aloft,
Bloom breathe, that one breath more
Earth is the fairer for.
Whereas did air not make
This bath of blue and slake
His fire, the sun would shake,
A blear and blinding ball
With blackness bound, and all
The thick stars round him roll
Flashing like flecks of coal,
Quartz-fret, or sparks of salt
In grimy vasty vault.

    So God was God of old;
A mother came to mould
Those limbs like ours which are
What must make our daystar
Much dearer to mankind:
Whose glory bare would blind
Or less would win man's mind.
Through her we may see Him
Made sweeter, not made dim,
And her hand leaves His light
Sifted to suit our sight.

    Be thou, then, O thou dear
Mother, my atmosphere;
My happier world wherein
To wend and meet no sin;

Above me, round me lie
Fronting my froward eye
With sweet and scarless sky;
Stir in my ears, speak there
Of God's love, O live air,
Of patience, penance, prayer;
World-mothering air, air wild,
Wound with thee, in thee isled,
Fold home, fast fold thy child.

GERARD HOPKINS

79.   A MEDITATION FOR
           CHRISTMAS DAY

CONSIDER, O my soul, what morn is this!
      Whereon the eternal Lord of all things made
For us, poor mortals, and our endless bliss,
    Came down from heaven; and, in a manger laid,
    The first, rich, offerings of our ransom paid:
Consider, O my soul, what morn is this!

Consider what estate of fearful woe
    Had then been ours, had He refused this birth;
From sin to sin tossed vainly to and fro,
    Hell's playthings, o'er a doomed and helpless earth!
    Had He from us withheld His priceless worth,
Consider man's estate of fearful woe!

Consider to what joys He bids thee rise,
    Who comes, Himself, life's bitter cup to drain!

A Meditation for Christmas Day

Ah! look on this sweet Child, whose innocent eyes,
  Ere all be done, shall close in mortal pain,
  That thou at last Love's Kingdom may'st attain:
Consider to what joys He bids thee rise!

Consider all this wonder, O my soul:
  And in thine inmost shrine make music sweet!
Yea, let the world, from furthest pole to pole,
  Join in thy praises this dread birth to greet!
  Kneeling to kiss thy Saviour's infant feet!
Consider all this wonder, O my soul!

SELWYN IMAGE

80. A MORNING SONG FOR CHRISTMAS DAY

[For Music.]

1 WAKE, what unusual light doth greet
    The early dusk of this our street?
2 It is the Lord! it is the Christ!
  That hath the will of God sufficed;
  That ere the day is born anew,
  Himself is born a Child for you.

Chorus.

  The harp, the viol, and the lute,
  To strike a praise unto our God!
  Bring here the reeds! bring here the flute!
  Wake summer from the winter's sod!
  Oh, what a feast of feasts is given
  To His poor servants, by the King of Heaven!

3 Where is the Lord?

2   Here is the Lord,
At thine own door.   'Tis He, the Word;
He, at whose face, the eternal speed
Of orb on orb was changed to song.
Shall He the sound of viols heed,
Whose ears have heard so high a throng?
Shall He regard the citherns strung
To whom the morning stars have sung?
Chorus.

Then wake, my heart, and sweep the strings,
The seven in the Lyre of Life!
Instead of lutes, the spirit sings;
With praise its quiet house is rife!
Oh, what a feast of feasts is given
To His poor servants, by the King of Heaven!

4 Who is the Lord?

2   He is the Lord,
That Light of light, that Chief of all!

3 Who is the Lord?

2   He is the Lord,
An outcast lying in a stall;
For in the inn no room is left,
While the unworthy feast instead;
He of all welcome is bereft,
And hath not where to lay His head.

1 What fitter place could I prepare,
What better cradle, say, is there
Than this my heart, if that were fair?

2 Thou hast divined!   A nobler part
   In man or angel, or of earth, or skies,
   There is not, than a broken heart;
   The which thy God may ne'er despise.

THE HYMN
Chorus.
Lord, in my heart a little child,
Now that the snows beat far and wide,
While ever wails the tempest wild,
                         Good Lord abide.

Nor go Thou if the summer comes,
Nor if the summer days depart;
But chiefly make Thy home of homes,
                         Lord, in my heart.

HERBERT P. HORNE

81.   CHRISTMAS AT SEA

THE sheets were frozen hard, and they cut the naked
     hand;
The decks were like a slide, where a seaman scarce could
     stand;
The wind was a nor'wester, blowing squally off the sea;
And cliffs and spouting breakers were the only things
     a-lee.

They heard the surf a-roaring before the break of day;
But 'twas only with the peep of light we saw how ill we
     lay.

We tumbled every hand on deck instanter, with a shout,
And we gave her the maintops'l, and stood by to go
    about.

All day we tacked and tacked between the South Head
    and the North;
All day we hauled the frozen sheets, and got no further
    forth;
All day as cold as charity, in bitter pain and dread,
For very life and nature we tacked from head to head.

We gave the South a wider berth, for there the tide-race
    roared;
But every tack we made we brought the North Head
    close aboard;
So's we saw the cliffs and houses, and the breakers
    running high,
And the coastguard in his garden, with his glass
    against his eye.

The frost was on the village roofs as white as ocean
    foam;
The good red fires were burning bright in every 'long-
    shore home;
The windows sparkled clear, and the chimneys volleyed
    out;
And I vow we sniffed the victuals as the vessel went
    about.

Christmas at Sea

The bells upon the church were rung with a mighty
    jovial cheer;
For it's just that I should tell you how (of all days in the
    year)
This day of our adversity was blessèd Christmas morn,
And the house above the coastguard's was the house
    where I was born.

O well I saw the pleasant room, the pleasant faces there,
My mother's silver spectacles, my father's silver hair;
And well I saw the firelight, like a flight of homely elves,
Go dancing round the china-plates that stand upon the
    shelves.

And well I knew the talk they had, the talk that was of
    me,
Of the shadow on the household and the son that went
    to sea;
And O the wicked fool I seemed, in every kind of way,
To be here and hauling frozen ropes on blessèd Christmas
    Day.

They lit the high sea-light, and the dark began to fall.
'All hands to loose topgallant sails,' I heard the captain
    call.
'By the Lord, she'll never stand it,' our first mate,
    Jackson, cried.
. . . 'It's the one way or the other, Mr. Jackson,' he
    replied.

She staggered to her bearings, but the sails were new and
    good,
And the ship smelt up to windward, just as though she
    understood.
As the winter's day was ending, in the entry of the
    night,
We cleared the weary headland, and passed below the
    light.

And they heaved a mighty breath, every soul on board
    but me,
As they saw her nose again pointing handsome out to
    sea;
But all that I could think of, in the darkness and the
    cold,
Was just that I was leaving home and my folks were
    growing old.

R. L. Stevenson

82.   UNTO US A SON IS GIVEN

GIVEN, not lent,
  And not withdrawn—once sent,
This Infant of mankind, this One,
Is still the little welcome Son.

New every year,
New born and newly dear,
He comes with tidings and a song,
The ages long, the ages long;

Unto us a Son is given

Even as the cold
Keen winter grows not cold
As childhood is so fresh, foreseen,
And spring in the familiar green.

Sudden as sweet
Come the expected feet.
All joy is young, and new all art,
And He, too, whom we have by heart.

ALICE MEYNELL

83.   NOEL: CHRISTMAS EVE, 1913

Pax hominibus bonae voluntatis

A FROSTY Christmas Eve
 when the stars were shining
Fared I forth alone
 where westward falls the hill,
And from many a village
 in the water'd valley
Distant music reach'd me
 peals of bells aringing:
The constellated sounds
 ran sprinkling on earth's floor
As the dark vault above
 with stars was spangled o'er.

Noel: Christmas Eve, 1913

Then sped my thought to keep
   that first Christmas of all
When the shepherds watching
   by their folds ere the dawn
Heard music in the fields
   and marvelling could not tell
Whether it were angels
   or the bright stars singing.

Now blessed be the tow'rs
   that crown England so fair
That stand up strong in prayer
   unto God for our souls:
Blessed be their founders
   (said I) an' our country folk
Who are ringing for Christ
   in the belfries to-night
With arms lifted to clutch
   the rattling ropes that race
Into the dark above
   and the mad romping din.

But to me heard afar
   it was starry music
Angels' song, comforting
   as the comfort of Christ
When He spake tenderly
   to His sorrowful flock:
The old words came to me
   by the riches of time

Noel: Christmas Eve, 1913

Mellow'd and transfigured
as I stood on the hill
Heark'ning in the aspect
of th' eternal silence.

ROBERT BRIDGES

84. NOËL

I

ON a winter's night long time ago
  (*The bells ring loud and the bells ring low*),
When high howled wind, and down fell snow
  (Carillon, Carilla).

Saint Joseph he and Nostre Dame,
Riding on an ass, full weary came
From Nazareth into Bethlehem.
  And the small child Jesus smile on you.

II

And Bethlehem inn they stood before
  (*The bells ring less and the bells ring more*),
The landlord bade them begone from his door
  (Carillon, Carilla).

'Poor folk' (says he), 'must lie where they may,
For the Duke of Jewry comes this way,
With all his train on a Christmas Day.'
  And the small child Jesus smile on you.

L

III

Poor folk that may my carol hear
   (*The bells ring single and the bells ring clear*),
See! God's one child had hardest cheer!
   (Carillon, Carilla.)

Men grown hard on a Christmas morn;
The dumb beast by and a babe forlorn.
It was very, very cold when our Lord was born.
   And the small child Jesus smile on you.

IV

Now these were Jews as Jews must be
   (*The bells ring merry and the bells ring free*).
But Christian men in a band are we
   (Carillon, Carilla).

Empty we go, and ill-bedight,
Singing Noël on a winter's night.
Give us to sup by the warm firelight,
   And the small child Jesus smile on you.

HILAIRE BELLOC

85.   A CHRISTMAS CAROL

THE Christ-child lay on Mary's lap,
   His hair was like a light.
(O weary, weary were the world,
   But here is all aright.)

The Christ-child lay on Mary's breast,
   His hair was like a star.
(O stern and cunning are the kings,
   But here the true hearts are.)

The Christ-child lay on Mary's heart,
   His hair was like a fire.
(O weary, weary is the world,
   But here the world's desire.)

The Christ-child stood at Mary's knee,
   His hair was like a crown,
And all the flowers looked up at him,
   And all the stars looked down.

G. K. CHESTERTON

86.   THE CREATURES' NOWEL

WHERE Mary keeps her court
   With the humble and the high,
The little dog has sport
For he is also by.

The creatures of the earth
They have great joy and mirth
On the night of the Great Birth.

The hedgehog and the hare
Are of that Birth aware,
Their timid footsteps go,
Quick, furtive, over the snow,

They come thro' the cold
The young Child to behold,
In the stable bare.

They have no fear there,
No hurt and no annoy,
But great bliss and joy
With the Baby Boy,
In that safe stable's shade
With none to make afraid,
To kill or to destroy.

The lamb in his white fleece
Plays with the wolf in peace,
The leopard lies down with the kid,
The ox and the ass they bid
The lion to share their straw;
All creatures tame or wild
Are there with the Little Child;
The ox says ' moo' and the ass ' hee-haw'.

R. L. GALES

87.   THE HEAVENLY NOEL

OH! what great thing is done to-night,
Or what good news has sped?
What ails the blessèd Saints in heaven,
They cannot rest in bed?
But up and down so ceaselessly
They go in joy and dread.

The Heavenly Noel

The gate-house all is lighted up,
Wherein Saint Peter dwells;
Saint James looks out of his great house,
All made of oyster shells;
In his good hostel by the flood
Saint Julian rings the bells.

Saint Catherine wears her silver shoes
And pearl-besprinkled gown;
Saint Barbara from her high, high tower
Upon the earth looks down;
Saint Christopher bends wondering eyes
On David's distant town.

The Angels' chanting sounds afar
An ancient waterfall;
They do not listen to their strain,
Nor answer to their call;
Their thoughts are on the little earth,
Not in the heavenly hall.

For there they see a lovelier thing
That is beyond the sky;
They see the little Lord of Heaven
Upon His hard bed lie;
Their hearts are filled with wonder for
The Change of the Most High.

R. L. GALES

THE Ox said to the Ass, said he, all on a Christmas
     night:
'Do you hear the pipe of the shepherds a-whistling over
     the hill?
That is the angels' music they play for their delight,
"Glory to God in the highest and peace upon earth,
     goodwill" . . .
Nowell, nowell, my masters, God lieth low in stall,
And the poor labouring Ox was here before you all.'

The Ass said to the Ox, said he, all on a Christmas
     day:
'Do you hear the golden bridles come clinking out of
     the east?
Those are the three wise Mages that ride from far away
To Bethlehem in Jewry to have their lore increased . . .
Nowell, nowell, my masters, God lieth low in stall,
And the poor, foolish Ass was here before you all.'

DOROTHY L. SAYERS

89.   CHRISTMAS CAROL

OH, brother Juniper, come out and play:
  Men should be gay on this Holy-Day.

Lo, brother Sun laughing there in the sky,
All so merrily, clear and high.

Blithe and merry are men and beasts all
In field and stall, in church and in hall.

Oh, little brother, let the fat men sneer,
We have good cheer this day o' the year.

Oh, brother Juniper, leave 'em their scorn:
Christ is born to us this bright morn.

J. D. C. PELLOW

90.

THE OXEN

CHRISTMAS Eve, and twelve of the clock.
   ' Now they are all on their knees,'
An elder said as we sat in a flock
   By the embers in hearthside ease.

We pictured the meek mild creatures where
   They dwelt in their strawy pen,
Nor did it occur to one of us there
   To doubt they were kneeling then.

So fair a fancy few would weave
   In these years! Yet, I feel,
If some one said on Christmas Eve,
   ' Come; see the oxen kneel

' In the lonely barton by yonder coomb
   Our childhood used to know,'
I should go with him in the gloom,
   Hoping it might be so.

THOMAS HARDY

HOW far is it to Bethlehem?
　　Not very far.
Shall we find the stable-room
　　Lit by a star?

Can we see the little Child,
　　Is he within?
If we lift the wooden latch
　　May we go in?

May we stroke the creatures there,
　　Ox, ass, or sheep?
May we peep like them and see
　　Jesus asleep?

If we touch his tiny hand
　　Will he awake?
Will he know we've come so far
　　Just for his sake?

Great kings have precious gifts,
　　And we have nought,
Little smiles and little tears
　　Are all we brought.

For all weary children
　　Mary must weep.
Here, on his bed of straw
　　Sleep, children, sleep.

How far is it to Bethlehem?

God in his mother's arms,
Babes in the byre,
Sleep, as they sleep who find
Their heart's desire.

FRANCES CHESTERTON

92.   EPIPHANY

WITH a long train of camels following them,
Laden with myrrh and frankincense and gold,
Balthasar, Gaspar, Melchior the old,
Draw near a stable door in Bethlehem,
And, bending down, each king his diadem
Lays at the feet of Him, whom they behold
Wrapped round in swaddling clothes against the cold:
The Babe that is a prince of Jesse's stem.

And the mild Mother sees with wondering eyes
The strange, bright gems on their uplifted hands,
Their jewelled swords, and raiment of rich fur.
And, drawing near beneath the starlit skies,
A train of camels bringing from strange lands
Tribute of gold and frankincense and myrrh.

FRANCIS KEPPEL

POEMS ON CHRISTMAS
MERRY-MAKING

93. NOWELL, NOWELL, NOWELL, NOWELL

*N*OWELL, *Nowell, Nowell, Nowell.*
    ' Who is there that singeth so *nowell, nowell,*
    nowell ? '

' I am here, Sir Christmas.'
' Welcome, my lord Sir Christmas.
Welcome to us both more and less,
           Come near.'   *Nowell.*

' Dieu vous garde, beau sire.   Tidings I you bring ;
A maid hath born a Child full ying [1]
The which causeth for to sing
        Nowell.

' Christ is now born of a pure maid ;
In an ox-stall he is laid :
Wherefore sing we all at a brayde [2]
        Nowell.

' Beuvez bien par tutte la company,
Make good cheer and be right merry ;
And sing with us now right joyfully,
        Nowell.'

94. MAN, BE JOYFUL.

*M*AN, *be joyful and mirth thou make,*
    For Christ is made man for thy sake.
Man, be merry, I thee rede,
    But be ware what mirths thou make :
Christ is clothèd in thy weed
    And He is made man for thy sake.

[1] Young.   [2] At once.

He came from His Father's seat,
　　Into this world to be thy make ;
Man, be ware how thou Him treat,
　　For He is made man for thy sake.

Look thou mercy ever cry,
　　Now and alway, rathe and late,
And He will set thee wonder high,
　　For He is made man for thy sake.

95.　　　　　　　MAKE WE MERRY

*M*AKE *we merry, both more and less,*
　　For now is the time of Christëmas !

Let no man come into this hall,
Groom, page, nor yet marshall,
But that some sport he bring withal !
　　For now is the time of Christëmas !

If that he say he cannot sing,
Some other sport then let him bring,
That it may please at this feasting.
　　For now is the time of Christëmas !

If he say he can nought do,
Then for my love ask him no mo,
But to the stocks then let him go !
　　For now is the time of Christëmas !

96

HOLLY AND IVY

HOLLY and Ivy made a great party,
Who should have the mastery
In landës where they go.

Then spake Holly, 'I am free and jolly.
I will have the mastery
In landës where we go.'

Then spake Ivy, 'I am loud and proud,
And I will have the mastery,
In landës where we go.'

Then spake Holly, and set him down on his knee,
'I pray thee, gentle Ivy,
Say me no villainy,
In landës where we go.'

97

ALLELUIA, ALLELUIA

ALLELUIA, *Alleluia,*
Alleluia, now sing we.

Here comes holly, that is so gent,
To please all men is his intent.
Alleluia.

But lord and lady of this hall,
Who so ever against holly call,
Alleluia.

Who so ever against holly do cry,
In a lepe [1] shall he hang full high.
                    Alleluia.

Who so ever against holly do sing,
He may weep and handës wring.
                    Alleluia.

98.   IVY CHIEF OF TREES IT IS

*I**VY** chief of trees it is,*
  Veni coronaberis.

The most worthy she is in town ;
    He that saith other, doth amiss :
And worthy to bear the crown ;
                Veni coronaberis.

Ivy is soft and meek of speech,
    Against all bale she is bliss ;
Well is he that may her reach ;
                Veni coronaberis.

Ivy is green, with colour bright,
    Of all trees best she is ;
And that I prove well now by right.
                Veni coronaberis.

Ivy beareth berries black ;
    God grant us all his bliss !
For there shall we nothing lack.
                Veni coronaberis.

[1] Basket.

160

NAY, ivy, nay,
  It shall not be, i-wis; [1]
Let holly have the mastery,
  As the manner is.

Holly stands in the hall,
  Fair to behold;
Ivy stands without the door,
  She is full sore a-cold.
            Nay, ivy, nay, &c.

Holly and his merry men,
  They dancen and they sing;
Ivy and her maidens
  They weepen and they wring.
            Nay, ivy, nay, &c.

Ivy hath a kybe, [2]
  She caught it with the cold;
So mot they all have
  That with ivy hold.
            Nay, ivy, nay, &c.

Holly hath berries
  As red as any rose,
The foster [3] [and] the hunter
  Keep them from the does.
            Nay, ivy, nay, &c.

[1] Certainly.   [2] Chilblain.   [3] Forester.

Ivy hath berries
 As black as any sloe;
There come the owl
 And eat them as she go.
     Nay, ivy, nay, &c.

Holly hath birdës,
 A full fair flock,
The nightingale, the popinjay,
 The gentle laverock.
     Nay, ivy, nay, &c.

Good ivy,
 What birdës hast thou?
None but the howlet
 That cries ' how, how.'

Nay, ivy, nay,
 It shall not be, i-wis;
Let holly have the mastery,
 As the manner is.

100.   HEY, HEY, HEY, HEY

*H*EY, *hey, hey, hey,*
 The boarës head is armed gay.

The boarës head in hand I bring
With garland gay in portering,
I pray you all with me to sing,
 With hey, &c.

Hey, hey, hey, hey

Lordës, knightës, and squïers,
Parsons, priestës, and vicars,
The boarës head is the first mess,
    With hey, &c.

The boarës head, as I you say,
He takes his leave and goeth his way
Anon after the twelfth day,
    With hey, &c.

101.   CAPUT APRI DEFERO

CAPUT apri defero,
  Reddens laudes Domino.

The boar's head in hand bring I,
With garlands gay and rosemary;
I pray you all sing merrily,
    Qui estis in convivio.

The boar's head, I understand,
Is the chief service in this land;
Look, wherever it be fand,
    Servite cum cantico.

Be glad, lords, both more and less,
  For this hath ordained our steward,
To cheer you all this Christmas,
  The boar's head with mustard.

NOWEL, nowel, nowel, nowel,
  Tidings good I think to tell.
The boarës head that we bring here
Betokeneth a prince withouten peer
Is born this day to buy us dear.
                    Nowel.

A boar is a sovereign beast
And acceptable in every feast:
So mote this Lord be to most and least.
                    Nowel.

This boarës head we bring with song
In worship of Him that thus sprung
Of a virgin, to redress all wrong.
                    Nowel.

103.   PROFACE, WELCOME, WELCOME

PROFACE,[1] welcome, welcome, proface,
  This time is born a child of grace,
That for us mankind hath take.
                    Proface.

A king's son and an emperor
Is comen out of a maiden's tower,
With us to dwell with great honour.
                    Proface.

---

[1] i.e. *proficiat*, may it do you good.

This holy time of Christës-mass,
All sorrow and sin we should release,
And cast away all heaviness.

Proface.

The good lord of this place entere
Saith welcome to all that now appear
Unto such fare as ye find here.

Proface.

Welcome be this New Year,
And look ye all be of good cheer;
Our Lord God be at our dinnere.

Proface.

104.   CHRISTMAS MERRY-MAKING

SO now is come our joyful'st feast,
    Let every man be jolly;
Each room with ivy leaves is drest,
    And every post with holly.
Though some churls at our mirth repine,
Round your foreheads garlands twine;
Drown sorrow in a cup of wine,
    And let us all be merry.

Now all our neighbours' chimneys smoke,
    And Christmas logs are burning;
Their ovens they with baked meats choke,
    And all their spits are turning.

165

Without the door let sorrow lie;
And, if for cold it hap to die,
We'll bury't in a Christmas pie,
   And evermore be merry.

Now every lad is wondrous trim,
   And no man minds his labour;
Our lasses have provided them
   A bag-pipe and a tabour;
Young men and maids, and girls and boys,
Give life to one another's joys;
And you anon shall by their noise
   Perceive that they are merry.

Rank misers now do sparing shun;
   Their hall of music soundeth;
And dogs thence with whole shoulders run,
   So all things there aboundeth.
The country folks themselves advance,
For crowdy-mutton's [1] come out of France;
And Jack shall pipe, and Jill shall dance,
   And all the town be merry.

Ned Squash hath fetched his bands from pawn,
   And all his best apparel;
Brisk Ned hath bought a ruff of lawn,
   With droppings of the barrel.
And those that hardly all the year
Had bread to eat or rags to wear,
Will have both clothes and dainty fare,
   And all the day be merry.

[1] Fiddlers.

Christmas Merry-making

Now poor men to the justices
   With capons make their arrants,
And if they hap to fail of these,
   They plague them with their warrants.
But now they feed them with good cheer,
And what they want they take in beer;
For Christmas comes but once a year,
   And then they shall be merry.

Good farmers in the country nurse
   The poor that else were undone;
Sour landlords spend their money worse
   On lust and pride at London.
There the roysters they do play,
Drab and dice their lands away,
Which may be ours another day;
   And therefore let's be merry.

The client now his suit forbears,
   The prisoner's heart is eased;
The debtor drinks away his cares,
   And for the time is pleased.
Though other purses be more fat,
Why should we pine or grieve at that?
Hang sorrow! care will kill a cat,
   And therefore let's be merry.

Hark, how the wags abroad do call
   Each other forth to rambling:
And you'll see them in the hall
   For nuts and apples scrambling.

Christmas Merry-making

Hark, how the roofs with laughter sound!
And they'll think the house goes round:
For they the cellar's depth have found,
    And there they will be merry.

The wenches with their wassail-bowls
    About the streets are singing;
The boys are come to catch the owls,
    The wildmare [1] in is bringing.
Our kitchen-boy hath broke his box,
And to the dealing of the ox
Our honest neighbours come by flocks,
    And here they will be merry.

Now kings and queens poor sheep-cotes have,
    And mate with everybody:
The honest now may play the knave,
    And wise men play at noddy. [2]
Some youths will now a-mumming go,
Some others play at Rowland-ho,
And twenty other gameboys mo,
    Because they will be merry.

Then wherefore in these merry days
    Should we, I pray, be duller?
Ho, let us sing some roundelays,
    To make our mirth the fuller.

---

[1] ? A see-saw.   [2] Cribbage.

And whilst thus inspired we sing,
Let all the streets with echoes ring,
Woods and hills and everything
    Bear witness we are merry.

GEORGE WITHER

105.   CEREMONIES FOR CHRISTMAS

C OME, bring with a noise,
   My merry, merry boys,
The Christmas log to the firing;
  While my good dame she
   Bids ye all be free,
And drink to your hearts' desiring.

With the last year's brand
  Light the new block, and
For good success in his spending,
  On your psaltries play,
  That sweet luck may
Come while the log is a-teending.[1]

Drink now the strong beer,
  Cut the white loaf here;
The while the meat is a-shredding;
  For the rare mince-pie,
  And the plums stand by
To fill the paste that's a-kneading.

[1] Kindling.

CHRISTMAS EVE: ANOTHER CEREMONY

COME, guard this night the Christmas pie,
That the thief, though ne'er so sly,
With his flesh-hooks don't come nigh
To catch it.

From him, who all alone sits there,
Having his eyes still in his ear
And a deal of nightly fear,
To watch it.

ANOTHER TO THE MAIDS

WASH your hands, or else the fire
Will not teend to your desire;
Unwash'd hands, ye maidens, know,
Dead the fire though ye blow.

ANOTHER

WASSAIL the trees, that they may bear
You many a plum and many a pear;
For more or less fruits they will bring,
As you do give them wassailing.

ROBERT HERRICK

106. THE WASSAIL

GIVE way, give way, ye gates, and win
An easy blessing to your bin
And basket, by our entering in.

The Wassail

May both with manchet [1] stand replete;
Your larders too so hung with meat,
That though a thousand, thousand eat,

Yet, ere twelve moons shall whirl about
Their silv'ry spheres, there's none may doubt
But more's sent in than was serv'd out.

Next may your dairies prosper so
As that your pans no ebb may know;
But if they do, the more to flow;

Like to a solemn sober stream
Bank'd all with lilies, and the cream
Of sweetest cowslips filling them.

Then, may your plants be prest with fruit,
Nor bee or hive you have be mute;
But sweetly sounding like a lute.

Next may your duck and teeming hen
Both to the cock's tread say Amen;
And for their two eggs render ten.

Last may your harrows, shears, and ploughs,
Your stacks, your stocks, your sweetest mows,
All prosper by your virgin vows.

ROBERT HERRICK

[1] White bread.

NOW, now the mirth comes
    With the cake full of plums,
Where bean's the king of the sport here;
    Besides we must know,
    The pea also
Must revel as queen in the court here.

    Begin then to choose
    This night as ye use,
Who shall for the present delight here;
    Be a king by the lot,
    And who shall not
Be Twelfth-day queen for the night here.

    Which known, let us make
    Joy-sops with the cake;
And let not a man then be seen here,
    Who unurg'd will not drink,
    To the base from the brink,
A health to the king and the queen here.

    Next crown the bowl full
    With gentle lamb's wool:
Add sugar, nutmeg, and ginger,
    With store of ale too:
    And thus ye must do
To make the wassail a swinger.

Give then to the king
And queen wassailing:
And though with ale ye be whet here,
Yet part ye from hence
As free from offence
As when ye innocent met here.

ROBERT HERRICK

108.   TO SIR SIMOND STEWARD

NO news of navies burnt at seas;
   No noise of late-spawn'd tittyries;[1]
No closet plot, or open vent
That frights men with a parliament:
No new device or late-found trick
To read by th' stars the kingdom's sick;
No gin to catch the state, or wring
The free-born nostrils of the king,
We send to you: but here a jolly
Verse crown'd with ivy and with holly,
That tells of winter's tales and mirth,
That milkmaids make about the hearth,
Or Christmas sports, the wassail bowl,
That tost up, after fox-i-th'-hole;
Of blind-man-buff, and of the care
That young men have to shoe the mare;
Of twelve-tide cakes, of peas and beans,
Wherewith you make those merry scenes,
Whenas ye choose your king and queen
And cry out: ' Hey, for our town green';

[1] An early club of Mohocks.

To Sir Simon Steward

Of ash-heaps in the which ye use
Husbands and wives by streaks to choose;
Of crackling laurel which foresounds
A plenteous harvest to your grounds:
Of these and such-like things for shift,
We send instead of New Year's gift.
Read then, and when your faces shine
With buxom meat and cap'ring wine,
Remember us in cups full crown'd,
And let our city-health go round,
Quite through the young maids and the men,
To the ninth number, if not ten;
Until the fired chestnuts leap
For joy to see the fruits ye reap
From the plump chalice and the cup
That tempts till it be tossed up;
Then as ye sit about your embers,
Call not to mind those fled Decembers,
But think on these that are t' appear
As daughters to the instant year:
Sit crown'd with rosebuds, and carouse
Till Liber Pater twirls the house
About your ears; and lay upon
The year your cares that 's fled and gone.
And let the russet swains the plough
And harrow hang up resting now;
And to the bagpipe all address,
Till sleep takes place of weariness.
And thus, throughout, with Christmas plays
Frolic the full twelve holidays.

ROBERT HERRICK

NOW winter nights enlarge
　　The number of their hours;
And clouds their storms discharge
　　Upon the airy towers.
Let now the chimneys blaze
　　And cups o'erflow with wine,
Let well-tuned words amaze
　　With harmony divine.
Now yellow waxen lights
　　Shall wait on honey love,
While youthful revels, masques, and courtly sights,
　　Sleep's leaden spells remove.

This time doth well dispense
　　With lovers' long discourse,
Much speech hath some defence,
　　Though beauty no remorse.
All do not all things well;
　　Some measures comely tread,
Some knotted riddles tell,
　　Some poems smoothly read.
The summer hath his joys,
　　And winter his delights;
Though love and all his pleasures are but toys,
　　They shorten tedious nights.

THOMAS CAMPION

To shorten winter's sadness,
  See where the nymphs with gladness
Disguisèd all are coming
Right wantonly a-mumming.

                              Fa la.

Whilst youthful sports are lasting
To feasting turn our fasting;
With revels and with wassails
Make grief and care our vassals.

                              Fa la.

For youth it well beseemeth
That pleasure he esteemeth;
And sullen age is hated
That mirth would have abated.

                              Fa la.

                              UNKNOWN.

111. THE DAMSEL DONN'D HER KIRTLE SHEEN

The damsel donn'd her kirtle sheen;
  The hall was dress'd with holly green;
Forth to the wood did merry-men go,
To gather in the mistletoe.
Then open'd wide the baron's hall
To vassal, tenant, serf and all;
Power laid his rod of rule aside,
And ceremony doff'd his pride.

The Damsel donn'd her Kirtle Sheen

The heir with roses in his shoes
That night might village partner choose;
The lord underogating share
The vulgar game of post-and-pair.
All hail'd with uncontroll'd delight
And general voice the happy night
That to the cottage as the crown
Brought tidings of salvation down.

The fire with well-dried logs supplied
Went roaring up the chimney wide;
The huge hall-table's oaken face,
Scrubb'd till it shone, the day to grace,
Bore then upon its massive board
No mark to part the squire and lord.
Then was brought in the lusty brawn
By old blue-coated serving-man;
Then the grim boar's-head frown'd on high,
Crested with bay and rosemary.
Well can the green-garb'd ranger tell
How, when, and where the monster fell,
What dogs before his death he tore,
And all the baiting of the boar.
The wassail round, in good brown bowls,
Garnish'd with ribbons, blithely trowls.
There the huge sirloin reek'd; hard by
Plum-porridge stood and Christmas pie;
Nor fail'd old Scotland to produce
At such high-tide her savoury goose.

Then came the merry masquers in
And carols roar'd with blithesome din ;
If unmelodious was the song
It was a hearty note and strong.
Who lists may in their mumming see
Traces of ancient mystery ;
White shirts supplied the masquerade,
And smutted cheeks the visors made :
But oh ! what masquers richly dight
Can boast of bosoms half so light !
England was merry England when
Old Christmas brought his sports again.
'Twas Christmas broach'd the mightiest ale,
'Twas Christmas told the merriest tale ;
A Christmas gambol oft could cheer
The poor man's heart through half the year.

SIR WALTER SCOTT

112.   WINTER WAS NOT UNKIND

WINTER was not unkind because uncouth ;
His prison'd time made me a closer guest,
And gave thy graciousness a warmer zest,
Biting all else with keen and angry tooth :
And bravelier the triumphant blood of youth
Mantling thy cheek its happy home possest,
And sterner sport by day put strength to test,
And custom's feast at night gave tongue to truth.

Or say hath flaunting summer a device
To match our midnight revelry, that rang

With steel and flame along the snow-girt ice?
Or when we hark't to nightingales that sang
On dewy eves in spring, did they entice
To gentler love than winter's icy fang?

ROBERT BRIDGES

113. BALLADE OF CHRISTMAS GHOSTS

BETWEEN the moonlight and the fire
In winter twilights long ago,
What ghosts we raised for your desire,
To make your merry blood run slow!
How old, how grave, how wise we grow!
No Christmas ghost can make us chill,
Save those that troop in mournful row,
The ghosts we all can raise at will!

The beasts can talk in barn and byre
On Christmas Eve, old legends know.
As year by year the years retire,
We men fall silent then I trow,
Such sights hath memory to show,
Such voices from the silence thrill,
Such shapes return with Christmas snow,—
The ghosts we all can raise at will.

Oh, children of the village choir,
Your carols on the midnight throw!
Oh, bright across the mist and mire,
Ye ruddy hearths of Christmas glow!

Beat back the dread, beat down the woe,
Let's cheerily descend the hill;
Be welcome all, to come or go,
The ghosts we all can raise at will!

Envoy

Friend, sursum corda, soon or slow
We part, like guests who've joyed their fill;
Forget them not, nor mourn them so,
The ghosts we all can raise at will.

ANDREW LANG

114.   CHRISTMAS EVE

Basil. Sandy. Brian. Menzies.

Sandy.

IN holly hedges starving birds
Silently mourn the setting year.

Basil.

Upright like silver-plated swords
The flags stand in the frozen mere.

Brian.

The mistletoe we still adore
Upon the twisted hawthorn grows.

Menzies.

In antique gardens hellebore
Puts forth its blushing Christmas rose.

Sandy.

Shrivelled and purple, cheek by jowl,
The hips and haws hang drearily.

Basil.

Rolled in a ball the sulky owl
Creeps far into his hollow tree.

Brian.

In abbeys and cathedrals dim
The birth of Christ is acted o'er;
The kings of Cologne worship Him,
Balthazar, Jasper, Melchior.

Menzies.

And while our midnight talk is made
Of this and that and now and then,
The old earth-stopper with his spade
And lantern seeks the fox's den.

Sandy.

Oh, for a northern blast to blow
These depths of air that cream and curdle!

Basil.

Now are the halcyon days, you know;
Old Time has leapt another hurdle:
And pauses as he only may
Who knows he never can be caught.

Brian.

The winter solstice, shortest day
And longest night, was past, I thought.

181

Basil.

 Oh yes! but fore-and-aft a week
  Silent the winds must ever be,
 Because the happy halcyons seek
  Their nests upon the sea.

Brian.

 The Christmas-time! the lovely things
  That last of it! Sweet thoughts and deeds!

Sandy.

 How strong and green old Legend clings
  Like ivy round the ruined creeds!

Menzies.

 A fearless, ruthless, wanton band,
  Deep in our hearts we guard from scathe,
 Of last year's log a smouldering brand
  To light at Yule the fire of faith.

Brian.

 The shepherds in the field at night
  Beheld an angel glory-clad,
 And shrank away with sore affright.
  'Be not afraid,' the angel bade.

 'I bring good news to king and clown,
  To you here crouching on the sward;
 For there is born in David's town
  A Saviour which is Christ the Lord.

'Behold the Babe is swathed, and laid
    Within a manger.'   Straight there stood
Beside the angel all arrayed
    A heavenly multitude.

'Glory to God,' they sang; 'and peace,
    Good pleasure among men.'

Sandy.
    The wondrous message of release!

Menzies.
    Glory to God again!

Brian.
    Again! God help us to be good!

Basil.
    Hush! hark! without; the waits, the waits!
        With brass, and strings, and mellow wood.

Menzies.
    A simple tune can ope heaven's gates!

Sandy.
    Slowly they play, poor careful souls,
        With wistful thoughts of Christmas cheer,
    Unwitting how their music rolls
        Away the burden of the year.

Basil.
    And with the charm, the homely rune,
        Our thoughts like childhood's thoughts are given,
    When all our pulses beat in tune
        With all the stars of heaven.

Menzies.

    Oh cease! Oh cease!

Sandy.

              Ay; cease, and bring
The wassail-bowl, the cup of grace.

Brian.

    Pour wine, and heat it till it sing,
      With cloves, and cardamums and mace.

    .   .   .   .

Brian.

    Hush! hark! the waits far up the street!

Basil.

    A distant, ghostly charm unfolds,
Of magic music wild and sweet,
    Anomes and clarigolds.

                        JOHN DAVIDSON

115.   NOW HAVE GOOD DAY!

*NOW have good day, now have good day!
   I am Christmas, and now I go my way!*

Here have I dwelt with more and less
From Hallow-tide till Candlemas!
And now must I from you hence pass,
    Now have good day!

Now have good Day!

I take my leave of King and Knight,
And Earl, Baron, and Lady bright;
To wilderness I must me dight.
    Now have good day!

And at the good Lord of this hall
I take my leave, and of guestës all.
Methinks I hear Lent doth call.
    Now have good day!

And at every worthy officer,
Marshall, panter, and butler,
I take my leave as for this year.
    Now have good day!

Another year I trust I shall
Maken merry in this hall!
If rest and peace in England may fall!
    Now have good day!

But oftentimes I have heard say
That he is loth to part away,
That often biddeth 'have good day'!
    Now have good day!

Now fare ye well, all in fere![1]
Now fare ye well for all this year!
Yet for my sake make ye good cheer!
    Now have good day!

UNKNOWN

[1] Company.

LATIN HYMNS

116. PUER NATUS IN BETHLEHEM

PUER natus in Bethlehem,
Unde gaudet Jerusalem.

Hic jacet in praesepio,
Qui regnat sine termino.

Cognovit bos et asinus
Quod puer erat Dominus.

Reges de Sabâ veniunt,
Aurum, thus, myrrham offerunt.

Intrantes domum invicem
Novum salutant principem.

De matre natus virgine
Sine virili semine;

Sine serpentis vulnere
De nostro venit sanguine;

In carne nobis similis
Peccato sed dissimilis;

Ut redderet nos homines
Deo et sibi similes.

In hoc natali gaudio
Benedicamus Domino:

Laudetur sancta Trinitas,
Deo dicamus gratias.

HEU quid jaces stabulo
Omnium Creator,
Vagiens cunabulo,
Mundi reparator?
Si rex, ubi purpura,
Vel clientum murmura,
Ubi aula regis?
Hic omnis penuria,
Paupertatis curia,
Forma novae legis.

Istuc amor generis
Me traxit humani,
Quod se noxâ sceleris
Occidit profani.
His meis inopiis
Gratiarum copiis
Te pergo ditare;
Hocce natalitio,
Vero sacrificio
Te volens beare.

O te laudum millibus
Laudo, laudo, laudo;
Tantis mirabilibus
Plaudo, plaudo, plaudo:
Gloria, sit gloria,
Amanti memoria

Domino in altis:
Cui testimonia
Dantur et praeconia
Coelicis a psaltis.

JOHN MAUBURN

118.   ADESTE FIDELES

ADESTE fideles,
Laeti triumphantes,
Venite, venite in Bethlehem;
Natum videte,
Regem angelorum,
Venite, adoremus Dominum.

Deum de Deo,
Lumen de Lumine,
Gestant puellae viscera,
Deum verum,
Genitum non factum;
Venite, adoremus Dominum.

En, grege relicto
Humiles ad cunas
Vocati pastores approperant;
Et nos ovanti
Gradu festinemus,
Venite, adoremus Dominum,

Stella duce, Magi
Christum adorantes,

191

Aurum, thus, et myrrham dant munera;
   Jesu infanti
   Corda praebeamus:
Venite, adoremus Dominum.

   Aeterni Parentis
   Splendorem aeternum
Velatum sub carne videbimus,
   Deum infantem
   Pannis involutum;
Venite, adoremus Dominum.

   Pro nobis egenum
   Et faeno cubantem
Piis foveamus amplexibus;
   Sic nos amantem
   Quis non redamaret?
Venite, adoremus Dominum.

   Cantet nunc hymnos.
   Chorus angelorum,
Cantet nunc aula caelestium:—
   Gloria
   In excelsis Deo:
Venite, adoremus Dominum.

   Ergo qui natus
   Die hodierna,
Jesu, tibi sit gloria
   Patris aeterni
   Verbum caro factum!
Venite, adoremus Dominum.

CORDE NATUS EX PARENTIS

CORDE natus ex Parentis
Ante mundi exordium,
Alpha et oo cognominatus,
Ipse fons et clausula
Omnium quae sunt, fuerunt,
Quaeque post futura sunt
    Saeculorum saeculis.

Ecce quem vates vetustis
Concinebant saeculis,
Quem prophetarum fideles
Paginae spoponderant,
Emicat promissus olim,
Cunctaque collaudent Deum
    Saeculorum saeculis.

O beatus ortus ille,
Virgo cum puerpera
Edidit nostram salutem
Feta sancto Spiritu,
Et puer Redemptor orbis
Os sacratum protulit
    Saeculorum saeculis.

Psallat altitudo caeli,
Psallant omnes angeli,
Quicquid est virtutis usquam
Psallat in laudem Dei;
Nulla linguarum silescat,
Vox et omnis personet
    Saeculorum saeculis.

O

Te senes, et te juventus,
Parvulorum te cohors,
Turba matrum, virginumque
Simplices puellulae,
Voce concordes pudicis
Perstrepant concentibus
    Saeculorum saeculis.

Tibi, Christe, sit cum Patre
Agioque Spiritu,
Hymnus, melos, laus perennis,
Gratiarum actio,
Honor, virtus, et victoria,
Regnum, aeternaliter
    Saeculorum saeculis.

PRUDENTIUS

120.   AVE JESU, DEUS MAGNE

AVE Jesu, Deus magne
   Ave Puer, mitis agne,
Ave Deus, homo nate
In praesepi reclinate !
O potestas, O egestas.
O majestas Domini !
O majestas, quidnon praestas homini ?

Ut me pauperem ditares,
Ut me perditum salvares,
Jaces pannis involutus,
Omni ope destitutus.
      O potestas, &c.

Inter bruta quam abjectus
Vagis, patris O dilectus!
Judex summe, verus Deus,
Propter me fis homo reus!
    O potestas, &c.

O mi Jesu, cor devotum
Post te trahe, sume totum,
Igne tuo sancto ure,
Ah ah penitus combure.
    O potestas, &c.

Procul vanas hinc amores
Procul malos arce mores,
Tuis meos aptos finge,
Aeterno me nexu stringe
    O potestas, &c.

121. NOWELL, NOWELL, NOWELL

*N*OWELL, *nowell, nowell, nowell,*
    Missus est ad virginem angelus Gabriel.

Angelum misit suum Deus omnipotens,
Ut unicum per filium ejus salvetur gens.
Virgo ave, clamat ille, O Maria clemens,
Concipies et paries, virgo semper manens.

Virgo clam tremescit, nam mira valde audit,
Eam cui est ille missus confortavit.
Altissimi Patris tui virtus obumbravit,
Cui per flamen sacrum gramen in te seminavit.

Nowell, Nowell, Nowell

Virgo clemens semper tremens ad verba angeli,
Cui flamen consolamen dat responsum illi,
Miti voce dicens, Ecce ancilla Domini,
Et secundum tuum verbum, ita fiat mihi.

Virgo Deum genuit verbum, quem alit cum cura,
Mirus Pater, mira Mater, mira Genitura;
Parit virgo solo verbo contra carnis jura,
Perseverante post et ante virgine pura.

Nobis natus, nobis datus, quem virgo lactavit,
Atque gregi, sic sub lege cunctaque creavit,
Miti corde nos a sorde moriendo lavit;
Miserere plebi tuae, Jhesu fili Davit.

Virgo pia, O Maria, pura ut lilia
Sponsa Dei, soror ei, mater et filia,
Tu Hunc ores, viatores ut fugiant vilia,
Et nos trahant huc quo gaudent sanctorum milia.

O Pater qui genuisti Hunc ab initio,
Et dedisti gentes Isti, pregaudens sacrificio,
Hic cum venit quos redemit sanguinis precio
Judicare, fac vitare nos a supplicio.

INDEX OF AUTHORS

197

INDEX OF FIRST LINES

Index of First Lines

Index of First Lines